Introduction

This boc............he.r............
and safety is................orkplace.................nents
can be mad............ig simple steps to.......u........effects
equipment, t.e w........ing environment o. sp......e tasks
have on health ar. safety.

Everyone plays an important part in safety at work. This book will help you to carry out your work activities more safely and in a way that protects your health. The book will also help you to understand the principles behind those health and safety issues with which you are not directly involved.

In some circumstances, even the decision-makers for your workplace need additional advice and information. In cases of a technical nature or where severe hazards exist, expert advice from suitably-qualified and experienced professionals is required.

Health and Safety: First principles focuses on good practice. It is not intended as a complete or authoritative guide to the law – employers, managers and the self-employed will require further information. Advice and information can be obtained from the relevant enforcement authority.

Chapter 1
A background to health and safety at work

Health and safety at work describes measures designed to protect the health and safety of people at work and that of others, such as visitors and members of the public, who are affected by work activities.

Key words

Accident – an unplanned, uncontrolled event with the potential to cause injury, damage or other loss.

Hazard – something with the potential to cause harm.

Health – a state of well-being, with the absence of illness or disease.

Health and Safety Executive (HSE) – the body that regulates health and safety and a major enforcement authority.

Health and safety policy – a document outlining an employer's general policy and commitment to health and safety. It will also include an outline of the organisation and people's responsibilities, together with arrangements for implementing the policy.

Occupational illness – health problems associated with work.

Risk – the chance (or likelihood) that a hazard will cause harm. In assessing the risk, consideration needs to be given to the degree of harm and the number of people who may be affected.

Safety – the absence of risks.

Workplace – any building or area where people work.

Workplace accidents and illness

There are hundreds of thousands of accidents in the workplace every year. In Britain alone, it has been estimated that 2.3 million people suffer from work-related ill health.

Official figures for workplace injuries in Britain in the year 2003 to 2004 show that there were:

- 606 fatalities

- 45,516 major injuries

- 130,247 injuries leading to more than three days' absence from work.

The statistics for fatal and major injuries cover members of the public as well as employees and self-employed people. The figures for absences of longer than three days relate to employees. In reality, the figures are likely to be much higher because many accidents are not reported formally.

Fatal accidents are most commonly caused by:
- falls from height (67)

- being struck by a moving object or vehicle (44)

- being struck by a moving, flying or falling object (29).

Major injury accidents are most commonly caused by:
- slipping, tripping or falling (11,269)

- falls from height (3,884)

- injured while handling, lifting or carrying (4,324).

Slips, trips and falls are a common cause of major injury

Absences of over three days are most commonly caused by:

- being injured while handling, lifting or carrying (52,422)
- slips, trips and falls (30,049)
- being struck by a moving, flying or falling object (14,780).

Other categories of accidents include:

- coming into contact with moving machinery
- coming into contact with harmful substances, such as chemicals
- making contact with electricity
- being injured by an animal
- becoming trapped
- various effects of fire, such as heat and smoke
- explosion
- drowning or asphyxiation.

Occupational illnesses – those linked to work activities or the workplace – include diseases and conditions, such as:

- stress, depression and anxiety
- musculoskeletal disorders
- breathing and lung illnesses, e.g. asthma
- skin diseases, e.g. dermatitis
- hearing damage
- vibration injuries.

Key points

- There are hundreds of thousands of accidents in the workplace every year.
- Common causes of accidents include:
  - poor lifting and carrying
  - slips, trips and falls
  - being hit by moving objects or vehicles.
- Various illnesses and diseases can be work-related, such as occupational stress, back pain and deafness.

The costs of accidents and illness

Accidents and illness cause a great deal of personal pain and suffering for individuals, as well as worry and financial difficulty for families. Employers have to provide temporary cover during staff absence and can lose money as a result of disrupted business activities. The indirect costs caused by the loss of customers and business opportunities, especially for the self-employed or small business proprietor, can also lead to hardship. A study by the Health and Safety Executive (HSE) showed that accidents cost up to 37 % of one organisation's profits.

Accidents and ill health can also be expensive for society as a whole. Another HSE study estimated an annual cost to society of between £20 billion and £31.8 billion, including medical costs, lost days' work and sick pay.

While there are certainly some direct costs involved in developing good health and safety standards at work – for example, in providing training and new equipment, there are huge potential long-term savings that can benefit individuals, families, companies and society as a whole.

Costs of poor health and safety standards

- Accidents, illness and stress.
- Deaths.
- Increased sick leave.
- Loss of production.
- Loss of earnings and increased personal costs.
- Bad publicity, resulting in a loss of reputation.
- Lowered staff performance and morale.
- Reduced company performance.
- High staff turnover.
- Prosecution, fines and imprisonment.
- Prohibition and closure.
- Compensation claims.
- Increased insurance costs.
- Legal costs.
- Loss of jobs.
- Treatment costs – first aid, etc.
- Costs to the health service and society as a whole.

Benefits of good health and safety standards

- Healthy, happy and motivated work teams.
- A safer working environment.
- Fewer accidents.
- Reduction in sick leave.
- A good reputation.
- Increased performance and profitability.
- Orderly working environment and procedures.
- Confidence in health and safety standards.
- Increased job security.
- Lower insurance premiums.
- Less chance of civil actions and compensation claims.
- Less chance of prosecutions.

Key point

- Apart from causing pain and discomfort to people, accidents and illness also result in financial burdens on employers and society.

The meaning of health and safety at work

Most people spend a significant part of their lives at work and do not expect their health to be damaged through work-related illness, disease or injury. Health and safety measures are concerned with controlling and reducing risks to the health and safety of anyone who might be affected by work activities.

Influences on health and safety

Various factors affect health and safety. They can be divided into three main groups:

1. Occupational factors – people may be at risk from certain illnesses or injuries because of the work they do, e.g. asthma from paint spraying.

2. Environmental factors – the conditions in which people work may cause problems, e.g. a noisy workplace can cause deafness.

3. Human factors – poor behaviour and attitudes can contribute to accidents, including error, carelessness, poor concentration, haste and ignorance of correct procedures.

Accidents may result from a combination of human error and faults in equipment or the working environment.

Key point

■ Health and safety is affected by occupational, environmental and human factors.

Achieving high standards

There will always be risks in the workplace, but they can be controlled by high standards of health and safety, such as:

- an effective management system and health and safety policy that set the standards and keep work activities under control

- good communication amongst everyone in the workplace and with other people that the business deals with

- positive attitudes towards health and safety, with everyone being involved and taking it seriously

- an effective risk assessment strategy aimed at reducing the likelihood of accidents and ill health

- buildings and equipment designed with health and safety in mind

- carrying out safe working practices

- good standards of cleaning and maintenance

- well informed and trained managers and staff

- an efficient reporting system for accidents, ill health and safety defects

- careful monitoring and the undertaking of remedial action to improve any deficiencies – a commitment to continual improvement in the workplace.

Good standards of cleaning and maintenance can help to reduce risks to health and safety

Summary

1. There are hundreds of thousands of accidents in the workplace every year.

2. Common causes of accidents include:

- poor lifting and carrying

- slips, trips and falls

- being hit by moving objects or vehicles.

3. Various illnesses and diseases can be work-related, such as stress, back pain and occupational deafness.

4. Apart from causing pain and discomfort to people, accidents and illness also result in financial burdens on employers and society.

5. Health and safety is affected by occupational, environmental and human factors.

6. Risks in the workplace can be controlled by effective standards of health and safety.

Key point

- Risks in the workplace can be controlled by effective standards of health and safety.

Chapter 2
Health and safety law

Most countries have developed legislation to protect the health and safety of people at work. In Britain, employers must take reasonable care to protect employees from the risks of injury, disease or death, while employees must take care to protect themselves and others who may be affected by their activities whilst at work.

Key words

Directive – instructions from the European Union for member states to pass laws specifying certain standards.

Enforcement authority – the organisation responsible for enforcing health and safety legislation.

Enforcement officers – environmental health officers, health and safety inspectors and others who are responsible for enforcing legislation.

Environmental health officers (EHOs) – enforcement officers from local authorities.

Legislation – a general term for laws, including acts, regulations, orders and directives.

Local authority – the local council.

Reasonably practicable – a legal expression that balances risk against the time, trouble, and money to prevent or reduce risk.

Welfare – issues concerning the well-being of employees, such as the provision of toilets.

Complying with the law

This chapter highlights some of the main issues that are controlled by health and safety legislation, although it does not cover every aspect of the law.

It is the responsibility of employers, the self-employed and those with specific responsibilities for health and safety to ensure that they are familiar with all the relevant legal obligations affecting their workplace. They must also ensure that they are sufficiently informed, trained and qualified to make decisions aimed at achieving appropriate health and safety standards. This may involve obtaining specialist advice and help.

Some aspects of health and safety might be covered by more than one branch of a country's legal system. In Britain, for instance, this means that a criminal court can impose penalties, including fines and imprisonment, when an individual or a company breaks a law. In some cases, it is also possible for claims to be made through civil courts for financial compensation for harm, injury or damage.

Legislation covers a wide range of health and safety issues

Key point

- It is the responsibility of employers, the self-employed and those with specific responsibilities for health and safety to ensure that they are familiar with all the relevant legal obligations affecting their workplace.

Work-related legislation

Legislation covers a wide range of health and safety issues. Laws in Britain tend to focus on one of the following:

- particular types of workplace, such as factories and construction sites
- a specific topic affecting a variety of workplaces and work activities – see list below
- general issues that affect every workplace, such as the management of health and safety.

Among the subjects covered by specific legislation are:
- workplaces
- work equipment
- safety signs
- electricity
- fire
- working at height
- highly flammable liquids
- display screen equipment
- manual handling
- hazardous substances
- noise
- personal protective equipment
- first aid
- reporting of injuries, diseases and dangerous occurrences
- consultation with employees
- health and safety management.

Legal responsibilities

Employers, employees and other groups have specific legal responsibilities for health and safety at work. These duties are covered by The Health and Safety at Work etc. Act 1974 (in England, Wales and Scotland) and by The Health and Safety at Work (Northern Ireland) Order 1978. These give legal responsibilities to:

- employers
- employees
- the self-employed
- designers, manufacturers and suppliers
- people in control of work premises.

Employers' duties

Employers must ensure that the health, safety and welfare of employees are protected, so far as is reasonably practicable. In particular, employers must:

- provide and maintain equipment and work systems that are safe and healthy
- deal with substances, such as chemicals, safely
- provide information, instruction, training and supervision
- maintain safe and healthy workplaces with the necessary facilities
- provide a health and safety policy statement when employing five or more people.

They must also ensure that workplaces and work activities do not put visitors, members of the public and others at unnecessary risk.

Employees' duties

Employees also have legal responsibilities. They must:

- take care of their own health and safety at work
- take care of the health and safety of others
- co-operate with their employer
- report dangerous situations to their supervisor or employer
- not misuse or interfere with anything provided for health and safety purposes.

Duties of people in control of work premises

People who are in charge of a workplace have legal responsibilities to ensure safe and healthy premises.

Duties of the self-employed

Self-employed people have the legal duty not to put other people at risk by the way in which they work.

Always follow instructions for the safe use of machinery

Duties of designers, manufacturers, suppliers and installers

These groups have legal responsibilities for the design and construction of articles, the use of substances, and the testing and installation of their work. They must provide adequate information, such as instructions for the safe use of a machine.

Key points

- Everyone has legal responsibilities for health and safety at work.

- Employers, employees, the self-employed, designers, manufacturers, suppliers, installers and people in control of work premises have specific legal responsibilities.

- Employees must:
  - take care of their own health and safety at work
  - take care of the health and safety of others
  - co-operate with their employer
  - report dangerous situations to their supervisor or employer
  - not misuse or interfere with anything provided for health and safety purposes.

The management of health and safety at work

The Management of Health and Safety at Work Regulations 1999 (originally 1992) (in England, Wales and Scotland) and The Management of Health and Safety at Work Regulations (Northern Ireland) 2000 have had a major impact on the way companies control health and safety standards.

Employers must undertake a range of tasks, including:

- carrying out risk assessments

- making arrangements for the planning, organisation, control, monitoring and review of health and safety measures

- appointing a competent person or persons to assist with health and safety

- establishing emergency procedures

- providing health and safety information and training.

Enforcement

Enforcement officers help to ensure compliance with the law. The Health and Safety Executive (HSE) is the enforcement authority for premises, such as factories, in England, Scotland and Wales. In most of the service sector, which includes shops, offices and wholesale and catering premises, enforcement is carried out by environmental health officers (EHOs) or technical officers from the local authority.

Until the formation of the Health and Safety Executive for Northern Ireland in 1999, enforcement in the province was undertaken by the Health and Safety Inspectorate and the Health and Safety Agency.

Enforcement officers have wide-ranging powers to help them to carry out their job.

They can:

- enter premises

- conduct investigations

- take samples and photographs

- ask questions

- give advice

- issue instructions – improvement notices and prohibition notices (*see* below) – that must be carried out by law

- initiate a prosecution.

Employers are often given the opportunity of putting problems right before formal action is taken. This may be done by giving verbal or written advice, but it is sometimes necessary to serve a legal notice.

Improvement notices

These specify that certain actions must be taken within a specific period of time. For example, a damaged floor must be repaired to remove a tripping hazard.

Prohibition notices

These are issued where there is a risk of serious personal injury. The notice may require a particular activity to stop immediately, such as the use of a dangerous machine, or it could even result in the premises being closed down.

Prosecution

Enforcement officers can start legal proceedings when offences have been committed. Prosecution is more likely when there is a serious health and safety problem or when somebody has ignored the officers' attempts to have health and safety deficiencies remedied. Prosecution is also likely if someone fails to comply with a notice.

Individuals, including company directors and members of staff, can be prosecuted as well as a corporate body, i.e. a company or organisation as a whole. Prosecution can result in unlimited fines, imprisonment for up to two years, or both.

Key points

- **The powers of enforcement officers include entering premises, carrying out investigations and serving notices.**

- **Prosecution for breaching health and safety laws can result in unlimited fines, imprisonment for up to two years, or both.**

Enforcement officers can enter premises and conduct investigations

Breaching health and safety laws can result in fines and imprisonment

Summary

1. It is the responsibility of employers, the self-employed and those with specific responsibilities for health and safety to ensure that they are familiar with all the relevant legal obligations affecting their workplace.

2. Everyone has legal responsibilities for health and safety at work.

3. Employers, employees, the self-employed, designers, manufacturers, suppliers, installers and people in control of work premises have specific legal responsibilities.

4. Employees must:

- take care of their own health and safety at work
- take care of the health and safety of others
- co-operate with their employer
- report dangerous situations to their supervisor or employer
- not misuse or interfere with anything provided for health and safety purposes.

5. The powers of enforcement officers include entering premises, carrying out investigations and serving notices.

6. Prosecution for breaching health and safety laws can result in unlimited fines, imprisonment for up to two years, or both.

Chapter 3
Health

Some dangers, such as trapping a hand in moving machinery, are easy to spot, but many health problems develop gradually. For example, staff may breathe in dangerous substances that eventually cause respiratory problems or they may strain their arms or back from working at a badly-arranged workstation. As many occupational health problems are irreversible, it is important to consider the possibility of health hazards in order to prevent them from causing illness and disease.

Key words

Acute – an effect on the body that occurs rapidly after a short exposure to a health hazard.

Carcinogen – a substance that can cause cancer in humans.

Chronic – an effect on the body that occurs after a long period of exposure or after repeated exposure.

Exposure – contact with a health hazard.

Health hazard – anything with the potential to cause ill health.

Hierarchy of controls – control measures listed in order of priority.

Occupational health – the activity of predicting and preventing work-related ill health. Also, health issues associated with work.

Health hazards

There are various types of health hazard:

- **chemical** – such as harmful dusts and liquids
- **biological** – such as infectious diseases
- **physical** – such as noise, heat and radiation
- **ergonomic** – such as badly-designed tasks, areas and equipment.

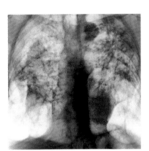

Occupational health hazards include respiratory diseases, such as silicosis

Badly-designed work areas can impact negatively on health

Key point

- Health hazards can be chemical, biological, physical or ergonomic.

Effects on health

The effects of occupational health hazards may be acute – occurring shortly after exposure to a hazard – or they may be chronic – occurring after a long period of exposure or after repeated exposure. Harmful effects include:

- skin diseases, such as dermatitis
- respiratory diseases, such as silicosis
- suffocation, such as through carbon monoxide poisoning
- cancer due to contact with a carcinogen such as asbestos
- disorders of the central nervous system
- damage to body organs
- blood poisoning
- birth defects as a result of contact with certain substances that damage human genes
- heat stroke through working in high-temperature environments
- work-related upper limb disorder, such as through repetitive movements
- work-related stress.

There are a number of ways in which hazardous substances can enter the body:

- **absorption** – where a hazardous substance gets onto the skin and is absorbed through it into the body and bloodstream.

- **ingestion** – through swallowing a hazardous substance or where one might be splashed into the mouth.

- **inhalation** – through breathing in a hazardous substance, such as toxic fumes.

- **injection** – where a sharp object, such as a needle, has a hazardous substance on it and cuts or punctures the skin.

The human body has many defences to prevent the entry of harmful substances. These include the skin and linings of the airways and gut. There are also defence mechanisms, such as coughing, sneezing, diarrhoea and vomiting, to expel harmful substances, while mucus and tears can trap particles or wash them away. Nonetheless, highly toxic substances, or high, long or repeated exposure, may cause illness and disease.

Key points

- Health hazards may cause a variety of effects, including diseases of the skin and lungs, bodily damage and disorders.

- Substances can enter the body by inhalation, absorption, injection or ingestion.

Preventing ill health from workplace hazards

It is important to identify occupational health hazards and to prevent them whenever possible. Good practice involves:

- identifying and avoiding health hazards

- measuring and assessing the hazards and risks

- applying control measures, such as good design, safe working procedures and/or the use of personal protective equipment/clothing

- regular reviews to check for changes.

Health hazards must be identified whether they are within the workplace or associated with work activities. If possible, hazards should be avoided altogether. Where this is not reasonably practicable, managers or proprietors must measure the extent of the hazard and risks. This may involve complex techniques and comparisons. In certain cases, government-set levels must not be exceeded.

Appropriately qualified and experienced professionals may need to be consulted for advice, such as an ergonomist or occupational hygienist.

Control measures such as good design can help reduce health hazards

Key point

- To prevent ill health caused by workplace hazards it is important to:

  - identify and avoid health hazards

  - measure and assess hazards and risks

  - apply control measures

  - review regularly to check for changes.

Control measures

If the hazard cannot be avoided, control measures must be put in place to minimise the likelihood of harmful effects and their consequences.

Some types of control measure are more effective than others. For example, a first and more effective measure might be to replace (substitute) a highly toxic cleaning chemical for a less hazardous one, but it may still be necessary to use gloves, goggles and other personal protective equipment. Nonetheless, this is better than continuing to use the original chemical while relying on personal protective equipment.

The list below shows various types of control measure. They are listed in order of priority and are sometimes referred to as the 'hierarchy of controls':

1. **Elimination** – can the hazard be eliminated?

If not, then:

2. **Substitution** – providing a safer alternative.

3. **Isolation** – moving a process to another area.

4. **Enclosure** – physically separating a process.

5. **Local ventilation** – removing the hazard directly from the process.

6. **General ventilation** – using normal room ventilation to reduce the hazard.

7. **Good housekeeping** – reducing risks from spills, dust and debris.

8. **Exposure time reduction** – reducing the time that people spend in contact with the hazard.

9. **Training** – to help individuals to reduce risks.

10. **Personal protective equipment/clothing** – to protect people on an individual basis (see Chapter 11).

11. **Welfare facilities** – to assist in minimising the risk, such as washing facilities.

Health surveillance and medical testing may also be necessary to detect early signs of ill health and to identify anyone who is particularly susceptible to a hazard and may need special consideration.

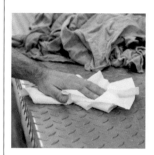

If a hazard cannot be eliminated you might consider substitution – for example, using a less hazardous cleaning method

Surveillance and testing can help to indicate the effectiveness of the control measures but should not be relied upon as proper safety controls because they can only detect – not prevent – ill health.

First aid and emergency facilities must also be provided. Again, these should not be relied upon as safety controls, although early treatment of symptoms will help to reduce harmful effects.

Staff should be given training in work-based hazards and risks and in the measures necessary to protect themselves and others. They also need to know about the possible harmful effects of their activities and to understand that they must report the first symptoms immediately.

Other management practices, such as regular inspections, supervision, good communication, maintenance and the identification of changes in the workplace or work tasks, must also be carried out to ensure that the control measures continue to reduce hazards and risks to an acceptable level.

It may be necessary to physically separate a process (enclosure)

Key points

- Control measures must be applied where health hazards cannot be avoided.

- If the hazard cannot be eliminated, then other measures must be considered, such as:

  - substitution

  - isolation and enclosure

  - ventilation

  - good housekeeping

  - exposure time reduction

  - training

  - personal protective equipment

  - welfare facilities.

- Health surveillance can be used to detect ill health and indicate the effectiveness, or otherwise, of control measures.

Summary

1. Health hazards can be chemical, biological, physical or ergonomic.

2. Health hazards may cause a variety of effects, including diseases of the skin and lungs, bodily damage and disorders.

3. Substances can enter the body by inhalation, absorption, injection or ingestion.

4. To prevent ill health caused by workplace hazards it is important to:

- identify and avoid health hazards

- measure and assess hazards and risks

- apply control measures

- regularly to check for changes.

5. Control measures must be applied where health hazards cannot be avoided.

6. If the hazard cannot be eliminated, then other measures must be considered, such as:

- substitution

- isolation and enclosure

- ventilation

- good housekeeping

- exposure time reduction

- training

- personal protective equipment

- welfare facilities.

7. Health surveillance can be used to detect ill health and indicate the effectiveness, or otherwise, of control measures.

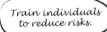

Train individuals to reduce risks.

Fill in bloody great big hole in ground...

Chapter 4
Safety – accident prevention

An accident is an unplanned, uncontrolled event which may cause major or minor injury, disease, illness, death, damage or other loss, such as delays incurring overtime costs. Safety is about not having accidents and reducing the risk of accidents and injury by putting in place appropriate control measures.

There are a number of ways in which people can be harmed through poor safety: electricity, fire and slips, trips and falls are three different aspects of safety that can all harm people in certain ways (*see* Chapters 5–7). In Great Britain, a system has been developed whereby certain accidents are reported centrally so that it is known where the greatest risks are and what the best way is of reducing them.

Key words

Accident – an unplanned, uncontrolled event with the potential to cause injury, damage or other loss.

Control or control measure – an item or action designed to remove a hazard or reduce the risk from it.

Reportable accident – an accident that must be reported to the appropriate enforcement authority.

Accident prevention

There are always reasons why accidents occur; they do not just 'happen'. It is, therefore, essential to:

- examine the workplace and all its activities to assess what could go wrong

- select safety controls to prevent accidents from happening

- examine what has caused accidents in the past and why

- implement health and safety measures and check them regularly to ensure that they remain effective.

A structured way to prevent accidents is called 'risk assessment', which is described in detail in Chapter 9. Risk assessment involves:

- identifying what can harm people and how

- assessing the existing control measures

- seeing if there is anything more that can be done to reduce the risk of harm.

Accidents where people escape injury are commonly called 'near-misses'. These should also be investigated to help to develop measures that will prevent future injuries.

Near misses should also be investigated

Key point

- There are always reasons why accidents occur; they do not just 'happen'.

Accident statistics

Accident statistics can be viewed as a triangle. The accident triangle shows the relative number of outcomes of accidents at work – from the rare accidents resulting in death to the most common incidents, or near misses, resulting in no injury. It is important to recognise that some of the situations that lead to incidents *without* injury could also lead to an accident *with* injury.

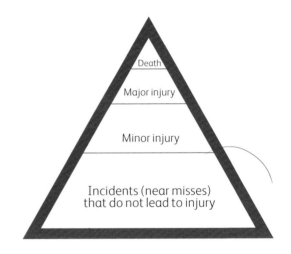

Causes of accidents

The following examples show how accidents can be caused:

1. A butcher cuts off his finger when cutting meat with a bandsaw

Possible causes – the butcher:

- selected the wrong type of equipment for the product
- used an unguarded or badly guarded bandsaw
- was using an unsafe working practice
- had not been properly trained
- was in a hurry because the shop was short staffed and a number of customers were waiting.

2. A customer falls down the cellar steps of a pub, causing neck and spinal injuries

Possible causes:

- the pub was badly designed, with the cellar opening off the main passageway next to the toilet door
- the manager had forgotten to lock the cellar door
- the customer had been drinking in the pub for three hours
- the customer mistook the cellar door for the door to the toilet because there was no sign
- there was no handrail and the steps were steep.

3. An employee's hand is trapped in a machine with hot parts, causing severe burning and crushing injuries

Possible causes – the employee:

- had removed the guards, allowing access to the dangerous parts
- was wearing loose clothing
- was chatting to his work mates.

Factors contributing to accidents

Many situations and actions can cause accidents, and a combination of several factors often leads to accidents that end in serious injury.

Factors that contribute to accidents at work include:

- poor design and structure of buildings
- poorly designed, selected, constructed, guarded or maintained equipment
- bad housekeeping standards, such as blocked gangways and spilled liquids
- poor lighting or ventilation
- lack of information, instruction, training and supervision
- dangerous working practices
- distractions and lack of attention
- playing games or practical jokes
- the use of alcohol or drugs, or both
- working while ill or tired
- no or poor supervision
- working too quickly
- ignoring rules
- wearing unsuitable clothing
- not wearing the correct personal protective equipment (PPE).

Accident reporting

Employers need to know that accidents have occurred so that they can prevent them from happening again. All accidents, including near-misses, and all health problems must be reported to supervisors or managers immediately by following the reporting procedure in the organisation. The management should then investigate the accident or circumstances to discover the cause, and set up appropriate controls to prevent health or safety problems from recurring.

All the important points about the accident, near-miss or instance of ill health must be noted in an accident book. The information is needed for the investigation and also provides a written record.

Some accidents must be reported to the enforcement authorities. They include accidents that result in:

- a death
- any type of injury, dangerous occurrence or disease that is specified by law
- an injury resulting in absence from work for more than three days
- a member of the public needing to go to hospital immediately.

Employers, the self-employed and others with the responsibility for reporting incidents should familiarise themselves with the relevant reporting requirements.

Key point

- Many factors contribute to accidents, and a combination of several factors often leads to accidents that end in serious injury.

Key points

- All accidents and work-related health problems, including near-misses and violence or the threat of it, must be reported to employers or the person in charge.

- Investigating accidents, near-misses and work-related health problems helps in the development of measures to prevent recurrences.

- Records must be kept of all accidents, near-misses and work-related health problems.

- Certain accidents must be reported to the enforcement authorities.

Co-operation and communication

The management of health and safety standards and the behaviour of everyone in a company both play crucial parts in preventing accidents and ill health. It is important that managers make health and safety one of their priorities and take the lead on establishing good practices. However, high standards cannot be achieved unless everyone in an organisation takes health and safety seriously. Everyone at work must, therefore, follow health and safety instructions and training and report any defects or problems. In this way, employees are then reliant on each other for their safety and wellbeing.

Some staff, such as safety representatives, are given additional safety responsibilities. Good communication between staff and management is essential and there are legal requirements for consultation and safety committees. Managers should consult staff during risk assessments and when plans are made for changes, such as re-designing the workplace.

Organisations with good health and safety records often use a variety of techniques to involve staff in health and safety issues. These include formal communications through a safety committee and informal day-to-day discussions.

Good communication between management and staff is essential

Everyone at work must follow health and safety instructions

Key point

■ Measures to help to prevent accidents and ill health include:

– examining the workplace and work activities to anticipate the causes of accidents

– controlling the environment, activities and specific hazards

– encouraging co-operation between everyone in a workplace

– following instructions and using safe procedures.

Summary

1. There are always reasons why accidents occur; they do not just 'happen'.

2. Many factors contribute to accidents, and a combination of several factors often leads to accidents that end in serious injury.

3. All accidents and work-related health problems, including near-misses and violence or the threat of it, must be reported to employers or the person in charge.

4. Investigating accidents, near-misses and work-related health problems helps in the development of measures to prevent recurrences.

5. Records must be kept of all accidents, near-misses and work-related health problems.

6. Certain accidents must be reported to the enforcement authorities.

7. Measures to help to prevent accidents and ill health include:

- examining the workplace and work activities to anticipate the causes of accidents

- controlling the environment, activities and specific hazards

- encouraging co-operation between everyone in a workplace

- following instructions and using safe procedures.

Chapter 5
Safety – slips, trips and falls

Everyone is exposed to the risk of slipping, tripping and falling regardless of where they work. Slips, trips and falls account for over a third of all reported accidents at work and are the number one cause of major classified accidents to workers. Slips, trips and falls are also a risk to the public, causing 50 % of all accidents.

Key words

Fall – where a slip or a trip causes a person who was upright (walking or running) to fall to the ground or floor surface.

Slip – a term used to describe where the surface of footwear (or the sole of the foot) loses grip with the floor surface.

Trip – where an obstruction or uneven surface causes the foot or leg to 'catch' the obstruction, making a person lose balance.

Causes of slips, trips and falls

The main reasons for slips, trips and falls include:

- wet floors
- stairs that are damaged; in particular, the tread (flat surface) and the nosing (the very front edging of a step)
- obstructions and things left lying around on the floor
- trailing cables and wires
- worn carpets, rugs and mats placed in the wrong place
- floor surfaces that are holed, cracked, uneven or damaged in some other way
- poor lighting
- wearing the wrong type of footwear
- people's behaviour, e.g. running instead of walking, carrying too much and obstructing the view ahead (which is more of a risk on stairs)
- using chairs instead of stepladders or proper foot stools.

Walk don't run

Use a step ladder or proper foot stool not a chair

Key point

- Slips, trips and falls are a major risk and cause of accidents.

Control measures

Slips are very difficult to control in certain environments, such as in swimming pools and kitchens where – for hygiene reasons – floors need to be keep quite smooth and may become slippery. The HSE has produced a slips assessment tool (SAT) to help to identify risk areas. Equipment is also available that can measure how slippery a surface is by measuring its 'roughness'.

Most measures to prevent slips, trips and falls are fairly simple and include:

- maintaining floors and floor surfaces in good condition

- keeping floors free from obstruction through good housekeeping

- covering or re-routing cables and wiring

- maintaining the premises and equipment to prevent leaks of water and fluids

- mopping up spillages as soon as they are spotted

- putting up warning notices and signs

- good lighting and having adequate space to do jobs

- wearing the correct footwear, including anti-slip soles for some workplaces.

- putting in place rules to follow for workers and the public, such as no running (always seen in swimming pools) and reporting of any slip or trip hazards they might spot.

While ensuring that floor surfaces and all environmental factors are as good as possible to prevent slips, trips and falls, much is down to human behaviour. If there are certain rules in place, such as no running or to wear a certain type of slip-resistant footwear, the advice MUST be followed. Otherwise, you may be prosecuted or disciplined by your employer; worse still, you may have an accident.

Cables and wires should be routed to prevent tripping

Mop up spillages as soon as they are spotted

Follow rules

Key points

- Good housekeeping is one of the best ways to reduce the risk of slips, trips and falls.

- Floors and stairs need to be kept in good condition and be well lit.

- Good, appropriate footwear needs to be worn and in certain areas, this will include footwear with anti-slip soles.

Summary

1. Slips, trips and falls are a major risk and cause of accidents.

2. Good housekeeping is one of the best ways to reduce the risk of slips, trips and falls.

3. Floors and stairs need to be kept in good condition and be well lit.

4. Good, appropriate footwear needs to be worn and in certain areas, this will include footwear with anti-slip soles.

Chapter 6
Safety – electricity

Electricity can cause electric shock, burns, fires and death. The fatality rate from injuries caused by electricity is high. It is, therefore, essential that electrical systems and equipment are designed, constructed, selected, maintained and used with care. Electricity is used in virtually every workplace – and even our safety systems may involve the use of electricity – so everyone must use electricity in the safest possible way.

Key word

Electric shock – where a current of electricity passes through the body's organs, muscles and nerves and may affect their function; for example, by stopping the heart.

Reducing the risks from electricity

It may be possible to remove an electrical hazard by using a manual tool. If it is not feasible to avoid the hazard or substitute equipment, it is important to find appropriate controls to improve electrical safety. Such controls could involve:

- **insulation** – to protect people against direct contact with electricity

- **earthing** – to provide a connection to earth, so protecting against contact with electricity

- **fuses** – protective strips of metal that melt and break if overheating occurs, stopping the supply of electricity and preventing overheating and fire

- **circuit breakers** – to detect excess flow of electrical current and stop the electricity supply to the circuit, provided that they are of the correct type and rating

- **residual current circuit breakers** – to protect against electric shock

- **voltage reduction** – so that the lowest possible voltage is used.

In addition, all cables, plugs and sockets must be suitable for their use.

The fatality rate from injuries caused by electricity is high

Key points

- Electricity can cause electric shock, burns, fires and death.

- The safety of electrical systems and equipment is improved by using insulation, earthing, fuses, circuit breakers, residual current circuit breakers and voltage reduction.

Design, construction and selection

If you are involved in selecting and purchasing electrical equipment, you should consider the following points:

- whether the design and construction suits the purpose required, especially the likely degree of wear and tear

- whether the item is designed to suit the environment in which it will be used, e.g. specially designed and constructed equipment is needed in wet or explosive conditions

- whether it complies with legal requirements

- possible additional risks from second-hand equipment

- the need to avoid adapters and trailing cables when the item is installed or in use.

Electrical equipment must comply with legal requirements

Key point

- Electrical equipment must be well designed and constructed and appropriate for its use. It must be installed safely and maintained and tested regularly.

Use of competent personnel

It is essential that systems are installed, checked regularly and maintained by competent, suitably qualified electricians or electrical engineers. You should never tamper with electrical equipment, attempt to repair it or remedy an electrical problem unless you have had specific training and have been authorised to do so. Qualified electricians must follow special procedures to prevent danger to themselves or to others.

Testing and maintenance

Equipment and systems that use electricity must be tested regularly and maintained thoroughly by competent personnel. The frequency of testing depends on a number of factors, such as the degree of wear and tear. Portable tools require extra attention.

Using electrical equipment

Organisations should establish safe working procedures, which should always be followed. Employers should ensure that employees receive full information, training and instruction on using electrical equipment safely and that they are supervised appropriately.

Always ensure that the power supply is turned off:

- when equipment is not in use (unless you have been instructed to leave it switched on)

- before opening, dismantling, maintaining or cleaning it

- when a fault, such as overheating, is evident or suspected

- before inserting a plug into a socket or removing it.

As water conducts electricity, you must ensure that you never:

- use electrical equipment in wet conditions (unless the equipment is specifically designed for the purpose)

- touch electrical equipment, switches, plugs or other electrical items with wet hands.

Key point

- General precautions include:

  - keeping the power supply disconnected when it is not required

  - keeping water and electricity apart

  - checking equipment before use and reporting defects immediately

  - using appropriate equipment for the task

  - using equipment according to the safety procedures of the workplace

  - using electrical equipment only if you have been trained and are authorised to use it.

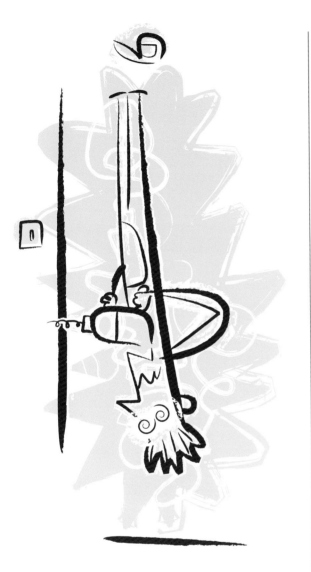

Reporting defects

Everyone who uses electrical equipment or works in an area where electricity is used must look out for problems and report them immediately. Some signs of a problem include:

- damaged sockets, plugs or cables
- evidence of overheating, such as burning smells or blackened sockets
- frequently blown fuses or electrical shocks.

Qualified and experienced personnel must then examine the equipment and make any necessary repairs or improvements.

Dealing with an emergency

A person who has received an electric shock may not be breathing and the heart may have stopped pumping blood around the body. The skin may be burned or look pale or bluish and there may not be a pulse.

In the event of an emergency:

1. Seek help. One person can ring for the emergency services while another assists the casualty.

2. Do not put yourself in a position where you could be electrocuted. Do not touch the casualty, but try to switch the current off. If you cannot break the current, stand on dry insulating material and move the person away from the electrical source using material that does not conduct electricity, such as wood, plastic or wads of paper. However, do not attempt this if high voltage supplies, such as underground or overhead power lines, are involved.

3. If you are a qualified and competent first aider, follow your training for dealing with electric shock. If you are not qualified, carry out any instructions given by the first aider and ensure that any other people in the vicinity do not put themselves in danger.

4. Obtain emergency medical assistance for the casualty.

In the event of an emergency, seek help

Key point

- In the event of an emergency, seek help and do not put yourself in a position where you could be electrocuted.

Legal requirements

There are legal requirements and official guidelines for the prevention of injury from electricity and the treatment of electric shock. Employers and the self-employed have a duty to assess what they need to do to comply with the requirements. Additional precautions may be needed for some activities and in some environments.

Employees have a legal duty to follow instructions and co-operate with their employer.

Key points

- Employers and self-employed have a duty to assess what they need to do to comply with legal requirements to prevent injury from electricity.

- Employees have a legal duty to follow instructions and co-operate with their employer.

Summary

1. Electricity can cause electric shock, burns, fires and death.

2. The safety of electrical systems and equipment is improved by using insulation, earthing, fuses, circuit breakers, residual current circuit breakers and voltage reduction.

3. Electrical equipment must be well designed and constructed and appropriate for its use. It must be installed safely and maintained and tested regularly.

4. General precautions include:

- keeping the power supply disconnected when it is not required

- keeping water and electricity apart

- checking equipment before use and reporting defects immediately

- using appropriate equipment for the task

- using equipment according to the safety procedures of the workplace

- using electrical equipment only if you have been trained and are authorised to use it.

5. In the event of an emergency, seek help and do not put yourself in a position where you could be electrocuted.

6. Employers and self-employed have a duty to assess what they need to do to comply with legal requirements to prevent injury from electricity.

7. Employees have a legal duty to follow instructions and co-operate with their employer

Chapter 7
Safety – fire prevention

Fire prevention is an important obligation for all businesses. Not only are people at work at risk from fire, but visitors, contractors, fire fighters, neighbours and anyone else in the vicinity may be affected.

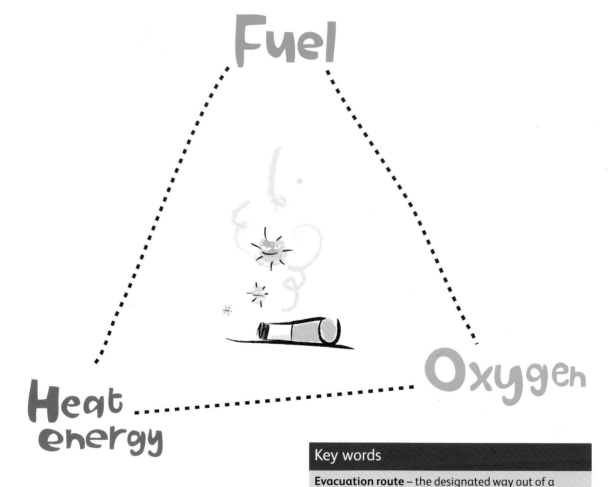

Key words

Evacuation route – the designated way out of a building in case of fire or other emergency.

Fuel – anything that can be burned in a fire, such as paper, wood, furnishings and flammable chemicals.

Fire hazards and the causes of fires

The key hazards associated with fire are:

- flames and heat
- smoke and toxic fumes
- reduced oxygen
- collapse of buildings.

They may result in injury and death, possibly with many fatalities.

Fires may be caused in a variety of ways:

- sparks from electrical equipment
- overheated equipment
- hot surfaces, such as lighting and heating equipment
- tools or equipment with a naked flame
- hot liquids, such as fat in fryers
- smoking
- arson.

There are many potential causes of fire including hot liquids, such as fat

Key point

- Fire can cause damage, injury and death.

Fire prevention

Fire prevention and control depend on managing three factors, commonly referred to as the 'fire triangle' – fuel, oxygen and heat energy. Fires need the right combination of these three to burn.

Once a fire has started it may spread very quickly, producing smoke and toxic fumes. The emphasis must always be on preventing a fire from starting, rather than on putting it out. Fire risk assessments help employers to consider how to prevent fires.

Control of fuel

Material which could become fuel, either intentionally or by accident, must be kept to a minimum; for example, waste and rubbish should be removed regularly, the storage of flammable substances should be avoided or kept to the minimum and dusty atmospheres must be well ventilated. Fuel must be kept well away – and protected – from sources of ignition; for example, flammable substances must be kept in properly designed and selected fireproof stores or enclosures. Sources of ignition should be kept away from fuels; for example, smoking should be banned in paper stores and near stores of liquefied petroleum gas.

Control of oxygen

It is not usually possible to control the oxygen in the air, but fires can be put out by smothering them as this restricts the supply of oxygen that a fire needs to continue burning.

Control of heat

Excessive heat and naked flames may start fires. These may be produced by friction in machines, hot surfaces, smoking, gas cookers and open fires.

Key point

- It is essential to maintain systems for fire prevention:

  – control sources of ignition

  – control fuels

  – avoid sources of ignition and fuels coming together.

Detectors and alarms

Detection systems are available which, when linked to a warning device, give early warning of a fire. The systems may detect high temperatures, smoke, radiation or certain gases produced by a fire. Manual or automatic fire alarms normally give the warning of danger by a loud sound, such as a ringing bell. Fire alarms must be checked regularly to make sure that they are working properly and everybody can hear them. Employees and regular users of a building should be made familiar with the sound of the fire alarm and the alarm signal should be explained to other people on their arrival.

Evacuation routes and procedures

All buildings must have a safe exit in case of fire. Emergency exits enable people to get out of a building in the opposite direction from a fire. Escape routes in large buildings need to be planned carefully so that they do not become too complicated.

Additional fire safety measures need to be installed in some buildings to protect the escape routes. These may include fire doors, emergency exits and fire resisting staircases. Emergency exit doors must open outward to outdoors. They must not be locked unless strictly necessary. If they are locked, then there must be a safe emergency opening system that is labelled and explained.

There must be permanent signposting that clearly shows the way out in an emergency. Escape routes and fire doors must be kept clear at all times. Internal fire doors must be kept closed as they help to prevent flames and smoke from spreading and limit the air supply to the fire.

There should also be an emergency lighting system that is checked regularly and maintained. Lifts must not be used as part of an evacuation route or during a fire because of the risk of people becoming trapped.

Managers need to know who is in a building, so staff, visitors and others should be asked to sign in and out. A register should be taken after evacuation to ensure that everyone has escaped.

Once evacuated, everyone should remain at the designated assembly point until told by someone in authority, such as a fire officer or senior manager, that it is safe to re-enter the building. Anyone who has to leave a building in an emergency should follow the instructions of the people in authority.

Escape routes must be kept clear at all times

Internal fire doors help to prevent fire and smoke spreading

Training and information

Everyone who uses a workplace should be trained what to do in case of a fire, explosion or other emergency. Where it is not possible to train people, such as visitors and contractors, a safety briefing should be given on their arrival.

Notices should be displayed at strategic points to give guidance on what to do in case of fire. Notices should describe the sound of the fire alarm, what to do when it sounds, what action to take on discovering a fire and where to assemble after leaving the building. Directions and diagrams should be provided in buildings where people may be unfamiliar with the layout, while translations into other languages may also be appropriate in some buildings, such as hotels.

Some staff may be nominated as fire wardens and given the responsibility for checking that everyone has been evacuated. They may be given extra training, such as fire fighting. On some premises, all staff must be trained in fire fighting because of the risk of fire or explosion.

Notices should be displayed at strategic points to give guidance on what to do in case of fire

Key points

- Detection, warning and evacuation systems, routes and procedures must be carefully designed and maintained.

- All staff should be trained in fire procedures and other people should be briefed.

- Escape routes must be kept clear and be properly signposted.

- Fire doors should be kept closed.

- After evacuation, everyone should go to the designated assembly point where attendance should be checked. Nobody must re-enter a building until they have been told it is safe to do so.

Key points

- Everyone who uses a workplace should be trained what to do in case of a fire, explosion or other emergency.

- Notices should be displayed at strategic points to give guidance on what to do in case of fire.

Fire drills

Regular fire drills should be carried out to check that the facilities and procedures are effective and that everyone understands what they should do. Remedial action must be taken if evacuation has been slow or incomplete.

Fire fighting

It is more important to evacuate people from a building than to stop and fight a fire. However, there are occasions when simple fire-fighting techniques can eliminate a fire before it takes hold, such as when dealing with burning fat in a pan.

Fire-fighting techniques, which may be automatic or manual, eliminate one of the factors in the fire triangle, such as by:

- starving the fire of fuel
- restricting oxygen, e.g. by using a fire blanket to smother a pan of burning fat
- cooling the heat.

Sprinkler systems

These automatically detect and control a fire at an early stage. They need to be permanently connected to a water supply and must be properly designed and maintained.

Hose reels

These are normally provided for use by the fire brigade. They must be easily accessible and should not be tampered with.

Portable fire extinguishers

It is important that any fire extinguisher used is of the correct type. Extinguishers are colour coded and contain one of a number of substances that can put out fires:

- **water** – paper, wood and textile fires
- **foam** – flammable liquids, paper and wood
- **powder** – electrical fires and most other types of fire.

When operated, pressure releases the substance that can be directed onto the fire.

It is dangerous to attempt to tackle a fire unless you have been trained how to use an extinguisher and have made sure that you can get out of the building.

Portable fire extinguishers should be fixed in suitable, accessible positions – usually by doors along exit routes – and must be clearly indicated by specific safety signs. There should be enough of them for the type of premises and risks involved in the work activities. Extinguishers must be regularly checked and maintained.

Sprinkler systems automatically detect and control fire at an early stage

Simple fire fighting techniques can eliminate a fire before it takes hold

Do not use a fire extinguisher unless you have been trained

Fire extinguishers

Category	Type
Water	A
Powder	A B C
Foam	A B
CO2	B

Key point

- It is dangerous to attempt to tackle a fire unless you have been trained how to use an extinguisher and have made sure that you can get out of the building.

Legal requirements

Various laws cover fire precautions and in Britain, some premises must hold a fire certificate. Employers, the self-employed and those in charge of buildings must familiarise themselves with the requirements that affect them. Advice can be obtained from enforcement authorities – in particular, the local fire authority.

Summary

1. Fire can cause damage, injury and death.

2. It is essential to maintain systems for fire prevention:

- control sources of ignition
- control fuels
- avoid sources of ignition and fuels coming together.

3. Detection, warning and evacuation systems, routes and procedures must be carefully designed and maintained.

4. All staff should be trained in fire procedures and other people should be briefed.

5. Escape routes must be kept clear and be properly signposted.

6. Fire doors should be kept closed.

7. After evacuation, everyone should go to the designated assembly point where attendance should be checked. Nobody must re-enter a building until they have been told it is safe to do so.

8. Everyone who uses a workplace should be trained what to do in case of a fire, explosion or other emergency.

9. Notices should be displayed at strategic points to give guidance on what to do in case of fire.

10. It is dangerous to attempt to tackle a fire unless you have been trained how to use an extinguisher and have made sure that you can get out of the building.

Chapter 8
Welfare

Welfare is not just health and safety – it is about a person's well-being at work. Employers have to provide welfare facilities, such as toilets, washing facilities, drinking water and places to rest.

There are also some general issues that can affect health and safety in all workplaces – for example, smoking, the use of alcohol and drugs, stress and the threat of, or actual, violence.

First aid is the first help given to someone to prevent an injury or illness from becoming worse. First aid can save lives, so there must be enough suitable equipment, facilities and designated personnel in every workplace to deal with cases of injury or illness.

Employers must provide welfare facilities

Welfare facilities

Every workplace must provide:

■ an adequate number of toilets that are kept clean, well lit and ventilated

■ washing facilities with hot and cold water, soap and hand-drying facilities

■ a supply of drinking water

■ facilities for storing clothing and, where necessary, changing facilities

■ facilities for staff during work breaks – this may mean providing seating, separate eating areas and smoking areas

■ suitable rest facilities for pregnant women and nursing mothers.

Smoking

Smoke in the atmosphere can be considered a form of air pollution. Research has linked passive smoking to lung cancer in non-smokers, irritation of the respiratory system and other harmful effects. It is, therefore, important that everyone at work should comply with company policies and restrictions on smoking – for example, by using only designated areas for smoking. In some workplaces, smoking must be banned altogether because of the danger of fire or explosion, such as where flammable chemicals are used.

Smoking causes air pollution and has a harmful effect on smokers and non-smokers

Stress

Stress creates the production of hormones in the body which have physical effects. A certain amount of stress may help us to perform tasks to the best of our abilities, but excessive stress for long periods can cause tiredness, anxiety and various physical symptoms. Health problems that have been linked to stress include stomach and skin conditions, heart disease and depression.

Various factors have been shown to increase stress levels, such as working in poor or cramped conditions, lack of communication with managers, overworking, concern about the risk of injury or illness and lack of job security.

Employers can help to reduce stress levels by considering the causes and taking appropriate action, such as re-designing a job, improving working conditions, improving communication and providing support. Individuals may be able to help to decrease their stress levels by modifying their lifestyles and improving their fitness, while others may find relaxation techniques helpful.

Alcohol

Alcohol increases the time taken to react to a situation, affects behaviour and reduces performance on jobs, such as driving or operating dangerous machinery.

Many employers have strict policies on alcohol and drugs – for example, staff may be banned from drinking at work, during breaks and before starting work. The policy may be supported by testing for alcohol with the employee's consent. It is important to remember that levels of alcohol in the body may still be high the morning after drinking the previous evening.

Excessive alcohol consumption is normally viewed as a condition that can be treated, with the individual's co-operation, and employers may encourage people with a drink problem to seek professional help. However, as a last resort, employers may have to take disciplinary action, possibly even dismissing someone, to protect the drinker and others whose safety may be put at risk.

Alcohol can jeopardise the safety of an individual and his/her colleagues

Drugs

Substance abuse, the use of illegal drugs or the misuse of prescription drugs may cause health problems and can cause safety risks in the workplace. Many drugs are particularly dangerous because they can change people's moods and perceptions. It is important to check that prescribed drugs will not affect performance at work. If there is an increased risk to safety, staff should tell their manager or supervisor. Suitable arrangements can then be taken to protect everyone's safety.

Employers must not ignore drug abuse but should take action to help the person involved and to protect others from safety hazards that could occur as a result of the abuse.

Employers must take action to protect employees from safety hazards arising from substance abuse

Key point

■ Alcohol and drugs have an adverse effect on the body, affecting judgement and increasing the risk of accidents and injury.

Violence

Verbal abuse, threats or assault can cause stress and anxiety as well as physical injury. Staff should always report violence, including verbal abuse, to their managers who should record and investigate the incident and, if necessary, report it to the relevant enforcement authority. As with other hazardous situations, employers and the self-employed should carry out risk assessments and put in place appropriate controls.

These could include measures such as improving the design of buildings to help create a more calming environment, giving staff training and information on how to deal with potentially difficult situations, re-designing jobs and reducing the handling of cash.

Key point

■ Employees who are subject to violence must report it.

Harassment and bullying

It is illegal under the Health and Safety at Work etc. Act 1974 for an employee to bully or harass another employee. The effects of bullying cause those who are bullied a huge amount of anxiety or distress, which can often be one of the causes for absenteeism from work and contribute to stress.

Employers need to have a policy in place to make it clear that harassment and bullying is unacceptable and is something that would lead to disciplinary action. Any policy will also make sure that there is a responsible person to go to if anyone is being harassed or bullied.

Key point

■ Harassment and bullying is illegal and can cause anxiety and stress.

First aid provision

Risk assessments must be carried out to show the level of first aid provision needed. The minimum provision is a suitably stocked first aid kit and an 'appointed person' (*see* below). Various factors affect the level of risk and the requirements for first aid, such as:

- working with hazardous substances or dangerous equipment
- the number of people
- people with special needs or inexperienced workers
- work in remote areas
- work that involves regular travel
- lone or shift work
- interaction with staff from another company or organisation, or the presence of members of the public.

In some workplaces and circumstances, it may be necessary to provide more than the required minimum. This could involve training additional first aiders or providing extra first aid kits, mobile telephones or a first aid room. It may also be necessary to liaise with the emergency services – for example, to discuss special hazards.

Everyone at work must be made aware of first aid arrangements; for example, by instruction and notices.

Self-employed people must also make sure that adequate and suitable provision is made for first aid at work.

First aid kits

The contents of a first aid kit should be linked to the risks at the site. Additional items may be needed where there are specific hazards – for example, eye-washing facilities may be needed where certain chemicals are handled. Medicines or tablets must never be kept in first aid kits because only qualified medical personnel are allowed to dispense them.

Minimum contents of a first aid box

The following items are recommended where there are no special risks:

- guidance leaflet
- 20 individually-wrapped, sterile, adhesive dressings of various sizes
- 2 sterile eye pads with attachments
- 6 individually-wrapped triangular bandages
- 6 safety pins
- 6 medium-sized, 2 large and 3 extra large individually-wrapped, sterile, unmedicated wound dressings
- 1 pair of disposable gloves (as required under HSE guidance).

A minimum 300ml sterile water container should also be provided where mains water is not available.

The contents of first aid kits vary according to workplace needs

Appointed persons and first aiders

An appointed person must be available whenever people are working. The responsibilities include looking after the first aid equipment, making sure it is always available, taking control when somebody is injured or ill and calling the emergency services if necessary. An appointed person does not have to be a trained first aider although basic training is recommended.

First aiders must be specially trained and certificated by organisations approved by the Health and Safety Executive. They should give treatment only in the techniques they have been trained to carry out; otherwise, they could cause further injury. First aiders may need additional training where there are special workplace hazards.

The numbers of appointed persons and first aiders needed in a workplace depend on factors such as risk, layout and number of employees. It is recommended that provision should also cover non-employees, such as customers.

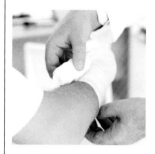

First aiders must be specially trained and certificated

Key points

- First aid prevents injury and illness from getting worse and can save lives.

- Adequate arrangements must be made for first aid, including responsible people, equipment and facilities.

- The exact first aid provision depends on the risks in the workplace.

- Employees should know what first aid arrangements have been made.

- An appointed person must be available whenever people are working.

Summary

1. Welfare facilities are required to maintain the well-being of persons at work.

2. Alcohol and drugs have an adverse effect on the body, affecting judgement and increasing the risk of accidents and injury.

3. Employees who are subject to violence must report it.

4. Harassment and bullying is illegal and can cause anxiety and stress.

5. First aid prevents injury and illness from getting worse and can save lives.

6. Adequate arrangements must be made for first aid, including responsible people, equipment and facilities.

7. The exact first aid provision depends on the risks in the workplace.

8. Employees should know what first aid arrangements have been made.

9. An appointed person must be available whenever people are working.

Chapter 9
Risk assessment

Risk assessment is a technique for preventing accidents and ill health by helping people to think about what could go wrong and ways to prevent problems. Risk assessment is good practice and a legal requirement. It often enables organisations to reduce the costs associated with accidents and ill health and to help them to decide their priorities, highlight training needs and assist with quality assurance programmes.

Hazards and risks

To discover how risk assessment works, it is important to understand the terms 'hazard' and 'risk'.

Hazards

A hazard is anything with the potential to cause harm. A range of hazards can be found in any workplace. Examples include:

- fire
- electricity
- harmful substances
- sharp tools
- noise
- damaged flooring.

Damaged flooring is a hazard – it has the potential to cause harm

Risks

A risk is the likelihood that a hazard will cause harm. Risk depends on a number of factors. For example, the risk of tripping on a damaged floor surface will depend on:

- the extent of damage
- the number of people walking over it
- the number of times they walk over it
- whether they are wearing sensible shoes
- the level of lighting.

Control measures

Hazards in the workplace should be removed whenever possible. Using the example of the damaged floor, this would mean repairing the damage. Sometimes, however, there is no alternative but to keep a hazard. In such cases, it is important to reduce the risk – the likelihood of an accident – by introducing appropriate control measures. In the example about the floor, this could include placing a barrier around the damage or putting up warning signs.

Carrying out risk assessments

Everyone carries out informal risk assessments every day. For example, before crossing a road, we stop and look. We estimate the speed of the traffic and consider factors such as bad weather and poor visibility. On occasions, we may decide that it is too dangerous to cross at that place at that time and we may move to a pedestrian crossing where risks, such as traffic speed and visibility problems, may be reduced.

Formal risk assessments must be carried out in every workplace. The assessors are usually specially trained, competent managers and supervisors who are familiar with the task or issue being assessed and suitable safety controls. They must also be up-to-date with relevant legal requirements.

The assessment process involves analysing tasks carefully to estimate the nature and level of hazards and risks. Staff are often asked to become involved in the process.

Formal risk assessments must be carried out in every workplace

There are a number of stages to carrying out a risk assessment and the people involved need to find answers to the following questions:

What are the hazards?

The workplace and activities must be carefully examined. Some hazards will be obvious, such as cables trailing across a gangway. Others may be hidden, such as access to dangerous parts of machinery during cleaning.

Who is at risk?

Everyone or only certain people in an area may be at risk. For example, a loud noise may affect everyone or only those working on a specific machine. Some groups of people may need special safety consideration as they may be more vulnerable to certain hazards – for example, pregnant women may be particularly at risk when lifting heavy objects, while young people may not be aware of all the workplace hazards and the need to follow safe procedures. Specific risk assessments need to be carried out for young persons and for pregnant women.

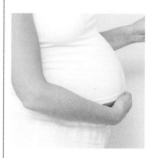

Specific risk assessments should be carried out for pregnant women and young persons

How big is the risk?

Three questions are necessary here:

1. What are the consequences of injury or harm?

The consequences could range from a scratch to a death. The most severe hazards need the most urgent attention.

2. What is the likelihood of injury or harm?

Something that is very likely will need remedying before something that is unlikely.

3. How many people are affected?

Fire in a building could possibly harm everyone, but a trailing cable in an office might only affect one or two people.

Can we introduce additional control measures?

Where a hazard or risk is not already adequately controlled, it may be possible to introduce extra measures. Various types may be used, although it is always best to remove a hazard if this is possible. For example, it would be better to repair a damaged floor surface, so removing a tripping hazard, than to leave the surface as it is and put up a warning sign.

It is not always possible to remove a hazard, but it may be possible to separate people from it; for example, a guard can separate a machine operator from a sharp or hot piece of equipment. Sometimes it is possible to make a substitution, such as by replacing a dangerous chemical with a less hazardous one.

As a last resort, staff may be provided with personal protective equipment (PPE). For example, chain mail gauntlets could be provided for someone whose work involves cutting or ear plugs could be issued to someone working in a noisy area. However, it is important to remember that the hazard is not sufficiently controlled, even though people are protected (for more information about PPE *see* Chapter 11).

All control measures must be checked on a regular basis to ensure that they are working effectively.

If it is not possible to remove a hazard, it may be possible to separate people from it

What other action is needed?

Information and training on all hazards and control measures must be provided. Records of the assessments should be kept.

Risk assessments must be reviewed from time to time to ensure that the control measures continue to be appropriate. A review should always take place when changes are made, such as the introduction of new equipment. Managers and staff who carry out risk assessments need full training in the technique and the legal requirements.

Key points

- Risk assessment is an important technique that helps to prevent accidents and ill health.

- Risk assessment encourages managers and key staff to think about what could go wrong so that they can control the situation before accidents or ill health occurs.

- A thorough risk assessment programme can help to improve operational efficiency, offer financial savings and maintain business reputations.

Summary

1. A hazard is anything with the potential to cause harm.

2. A risk is the likelihood that that a hazard will cause harm.

3. Control measures can help to reduce risk.

4. Risk assessment is an important technique that helps to prevent accidents and ill health.

5. Risk assessment encourages managers and key staff to think about what could go wrong so that they can control the situation before accidents or ill health occurs.

6. A thorough risk assessment programme can help to improve operational efficiency, offer financial savings and maintain business reputations.

Chapter 10
The workplace

The workplace itself can create risks to people at work, as can the equipment and machinery used in them. There are numerous types of workplace, including offices, shops, factories, hotels, catering establishments, places of entertainment, hospitals and educational establishments. Even though these premises vary, there are certain features and issues that need to be considered in every workplace to ensure the health, safety and welfare of the people who work there and anyone else affected by the work activities. While some people have specific responsibilities for buildings, everyone has a duty to keep the workplace in a safe condition.

Key words

Safety signs – specially-designed signs with the shape and colours having a particular meaning. The four main safety signs are: mandatory; safe condition; prohibition and warning.

Safe working procedures – the methods and the sequence in which people do things at work that have been devised to prevent and reduce the risk of harm to people who are carrying out a particular task.

Workplace – any place where people are working, including within buildings, while on scaffolding or ladders, outside or in a confined space.

Workstation – the particular place (and equipment used) where anyone might work; for example, at a desk with display screen equipment or a woodworking machine cutting pieces of wood.

Design, layout and space

A good design and effective layout are essential in every workplace and the design should take into account the likely hazards of the work activities.

There must be enough space for people to be able to do their jobs safely. Cramped conditions can result in accidents, particularly if people are working with sharp tools or chemicals, or if they are involved in other hazardous activities.

There should also be enough space for people and vehicles to move around easily (see Chapter 16). People must also be protected from other hazards, such as exhaust fumes and falling loads.

Appropriate safety precautions must be provided wherever there are hazardous areas, such as loading bays, pits, ladders, platforms and roofs. Falls and/or crushes may result in severe injury or death. Wherever possible, they should be prevented by physical means, such as rails and guards. Working at height is covered in more detail in Chapter 15.

Key points

- Everyone has a responsibility for keeping the workplace in a safe condition.

- Workplaces must be designed with safety in mind.

- People should have enough space to work comfortably, without being put at unnecessary risk.

Structure

Buildings must be solid, secure and constructed from materials that are appropriate to the work activities and their hazards, such as allowing for damp atmospheres, hazardous chemicals and the need for fire resistance. Fixtures and materials must be suitable and secure.

Floors

Floors must be strong enough for the purpose, with an even surface without holes and sudden changes in level. Anti-corrosion and non-slip finishes may be necessary in some workplaces.

Stairs, escalators and moving walkways

Staircases should be designed to enable safe use – not too steep or slippery and without any loose edges which could make someone trip. There should always be a handrail. Open staircases are best avoided or should at least be guarded.

Escalators and moving walkways must have various safety devices to ensure that they work safely. They should have at least one easily identifiable and accessible emergency stop control.

Stairs, escalators and moving walkways should be properly constructed and maintained.

Doors and windows

Various safety measures, such as sight panels, are needed for swing doors, while powered doors need safety devices to prevent crushing and trapping.

It must be easy to open and close windows and this must be possible without endangering other people; for example, where a window opens onto a walkway. The design must also make it possible to clean the window in safety.

Some areas of glass and other transparent materials need to be constructed of safety material or protected against breakage. They should be marked, such as with textured or coloured strips, if there is any risk of people walking into them.

Swing doors must have sight panels

Key points

- Buildings must be made from suitable materials, with good ventilation, lighting and temperature control.

- Areas such as stairs and gangways must not be overlooked for safety. Particular care must be taken where they are part of a fire evacuation route.

Services

All services should be designed with health and safety in mind.

Heating and cooling

The temperature at work should not be too hot or cold. The precise temperature set depends on a number of factors, including the type of work being carried out, the level of physical activity undertaken and the typical clothing worn. The recommended minimum temperatures are:

- 16°C for office work and similar non-physical activities

- 13°C where there is physical work.

Whilst there is no legal requirement for a maximum temperature in a workplace, a risk assessment should be undertaken if the temperature is felt to be excessive.

Where it is not possible to achieve a suitable overall air temperature, organisations should consider:

- insulating hot equipment

- increasing ventilation levels

- providing local heating or cooling equipment

- providing suitable clothing

- reducing the time that people spend in hot or cold conditions, for example, by job rotation or more frequent breaks

- providing those who are working in hot conditions with easy access to drinking water and changes of clothes

- providing information, instruction, training and supervision to ensure that necessary precautions are taken.

Organisations must also take into account, and minimise the risks from, the hazards associated with heating and cooling systems. These could include burns from hot surfaces, fire from overheated equipment and Legionnaires' disease associated with wet air-conditioning systems.

Ventilation

Good ventilation can significantly improve working conditions and efficiency. Natural or artificial ventilation, or both, is required to remove moist, warm or contaminated air and replace it with fresh air.

Lighting

Poor lighting is likely to increase the risk from other hazards, such as trailing cables. Adequate levels of lighting must be achieved everywhere in order to maintain safety and reduce eyestrain. Particular consideration should be given to areas such as stairways, gangways, entrances and exits. Emergency lighting should also be provided where necessary.

Where display screen equipment is used, such as in offices, lighting is very important and should provide minimum levels of glare and reflection on the display screen. At the same time, sufficient lighting is necessary to enable paper documents to be read and other tasks to be undertaken safely (see Chapter 12).

Adequate levels of lighting help to maintain safety – particularly in areas such as stairways

Maintenance and housekeeping

Buildings, facilities and equipment must be regularly and thoroughly checked and maintained to ensure that they remain safe.

All working environments must be kept safe on a continual basis. Rubbish and waste materials must not be allowed to accumulate. They should be kept in appropriate containers and removed regularly. The workplace must be kept clean and tidy, without any obstructions or blockages of walkways, particularly fire evacuation routes.

Storage and stacking

Many accidents result from unsafe storing, racking and stacking, so various safety measures must be taken. For example, there must be an appropriate design and construction using suitable materials. Measures must be taken to prevent damage, such as regular checking and maintenance, defect reporting, limits on loads and heights, careful working practices and training and supervision.

Keeping storage areas clean and tidy will reduce the likelihood of accidents.

Key point

- Buildings must be well maintained and kept clean and tidy. Rubbish should be removed regularly, walkways must not be blocked and stock should be stored safely.

Workstations and seats

Workstations and seats must be suited to the task and the person using them. Seats must give good back support and footrests should be provided where needed (*see* Chapter 12).

Special environments

Some workplaces present particular hazards because of their use. For example, swimming pools have slippery floor surfaces and a large volume of water, while construction sites have unfinished structures. Additional safety controls may be necessary as a consequence. Employers and the self-employed must make themselves familiar with their legal obligations and the recommendations for their particular working environments.

Procedures, training and supervision

Safe working procedures must be established. They are particularly important where the hazards are severe and the risks are great, such as in roof work or when using vehicles in the workplace. Staff must be given information, instruction, training and supervision appropriate to the hazards and safety procedures of the workplace.

Safety signs

Safety signs communicate information, such as warning of a hazard, showing the way to a fire exit or instructing employees to wear personal protective equipment. Regulations specify certain types to be used, helping to make them easy to recognise and understand wherever they appear.

There is a range of standard safety signs, including visual, audio (spoken and acoustic signals), hand signals and pipework marking. Safety signs must be displayed in appropriate places and kept in good condition.

The main categories of safety sign are:

- **warning signs** – for hazards, such as flammable materials
- **prohibition signs** – prohibiting certain actions, such as smoking
- **mandatory signs** – telling people that they must do something, such as wearing hearing protection
- **safe condition signs** – giving information about safety features, such as fire exits.

The colour and shape of the sign identifies its meaning.

Traffic signs and fire signs are among the others that must also be displayed in appropriate places.

Employers must explain the meaning of signs and ensure that everyone understands what action should be taken.

Warning sign

Prohibition sign

Mandatory sign

Safe condition signs

Summary

1. Everyone has a responsibility for keeping the workplace in a safe condition.

2. Workplaces must be designed with safety in mind.

3. People should have enough space to work comfortably, without being put at unnecessary risk.

4. Buildings must be made from suitable materials, with good ventilation, lighting and temperature control.

5. Areas such as stairs and gangways must not be overlooked for safety. Particular care must be taken where they are part of a fire evacuation route.

6. Buildings must be well maintained and kept clean and tidy. Rubbish should be removed regularly, walkways must not be blocked and stock should be stored safely.

7. Safety signs must be displayed where appropriate and staff must follow the instructions or heed the warning displayed.

Key point

■ Safety signs must be displayed where appropriate and staff must follow the instructions or heed the warning displayed.

Chapter 11
Work equipment

Equipment and machinery used in the workplace can create risks to people at work. As a result, it is often necessary for people to wear and use personal protective equipment and clothing (PPE/C) to protect themselves. PPE/C is an essential last resort in circumstances where hazards cannot be controlled in other ways. There are various types of PPE/C, including safety glasses and goggles, head protection, gloves, footwear, masks, breathing apparatus, ear defenders, ear plugs and outdoor clothing.

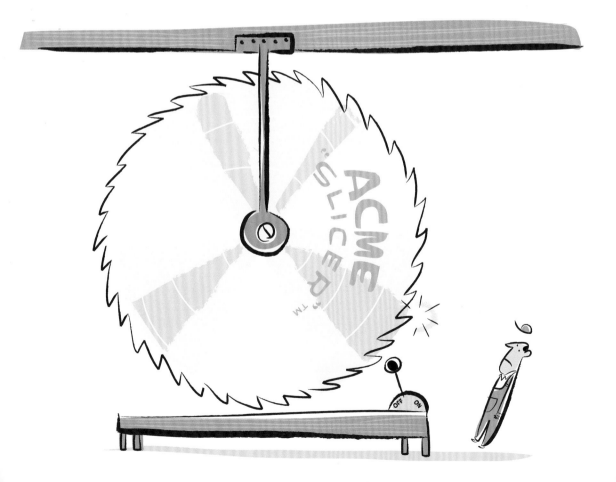

CE mark – an indication that equipment complies with European standards for design and manufacture.

Fail to safety – a mechanism incorporated into the design of a product that keeps the product safe even when something has gone wrong.

Personal protective equipment and clothing (PPE/C) – equipment and clothes used and worn to protect the wearer against hazards.

Respiratory protective equipment – personal protective equipment designed to protect the airways from inhaling hazardous substances in the air such as fumes or dust.

Work equipment – machines and tools for use at work. This includes equipment of all kinds, including photocopiers, drills, fork-lift trucks, ladders, food slicers and tractors.

Take care to avoid entrapment and entanglement and other hazards associated with work equipment

Key point

- The main dangers associated with machinery are entrapment, impact, contact, entanglement and ejection.

Hazards from work equipment

There are many hazards associated with work equipment. For example, hot parts and potentially harmful toner in a laser printer, sharp edges on cutting tools, rotating parts in a mixer, moving parts in a press, gas from heaters and fire from fryers. Machines can cause injury in five main ways:

1. Entrapment – where parts of the body, e.g. fingers, are caught in parts of a machine.

2. Impact – where the body is crushed by moving parts or by items being processed.

3. Contact – where the body touches sharp edges, hot items, live electrical items or abrasive surfaces.

4. Entanglement – where parts of the body, e.g. hair, clothing or jewellery become caught in parts of a machine.

5. Ejection – where parts of a machine or materials being used fly out and hit the body.

Preventing injuries

Many jobs involve the use of machines and most have associated hazards. However, a variety of actions can be taken to make equipment safer and reduce the risks:

Remove the hazard

The best methods of preventing injuries are by redesigning a task so that dangerous machinery is not needed or by eliminating hazards at the design stage. As this may not be possible, other methods have to be considered.

Minimise access to the hazard

If the hazard cannot be removed completely, it may be possible to make dangerous machine parts inaccessible or to improve safety by enclosing moving parts or by using automatic devices to feed machines. It may also be possible to restrict access to rooms with dangerous machines. All such machines should always be positioned safely where operators cannot be easily knocked or distracted.

Designed for safety

Good design and construction should:

- ensure the safety of machines by providing suitable operating controls that are easy to see and use

- provide operating controls that prevent equipment from being turned on accidentally

- incorporate a suitable emergency stop control

- ensure that a machine will 'fail to safety' so that, for example, it will not operate if there is a fault

- provide, where necessary, a means of disconnecting a machine from a power source

- minimise risks during maintenance and cleaning as well as during normal operation.

Guarding

Where hazards cannot be avoided, guards must be provided to prevent people getting close to any dangerous parts. There are different types of guard, including:

- guards fixed over dangerous parts

- guards that will not allow the machine to operate unless they are in place

- barriers to prevent people getting near dangerous machines

- devices that ensure that the operator's hands are away from danger.

Guards vary in their effectiveness and the people they protect, so they must be chosen with care.

When hazards cannot be avoided, guards must be provided

Selecting and purchasing equipment

It is important to select the safest possible option for any particular activity. Purchasing new machinery that is well designed and constructed is often a way of reducing the risk of injuries. If you are involved in the selection and purchase of equipment, it is important to:

- ask technical questions and compare the information provided by different suppliers

- check that the machine has a CE mark

- satisfy yourself that you have obtained all the relevant safety information

- ensure that there will be adequate training provision.

The work environment

To make work equipment safer to use, other issues must also be considered, such as lighting levels and the condition of the surrounding environment. Installation must be carried out carefully to ensure stability and safe operation.

Safe working procedures

Organisations must:

- use work equipment for the correct purpose and only in the manner specified by the manufacturer

- establish safe working procedures for all work equipment in line with the manufacturer's instructions and recommendations

- train and instruct operators properly

- supervise work with machinery

- ensure that safety procedures are followed diligently.

Safety procedures depend on the work activity and the work equipment used, but they are likely to include:

1. A ban on:

- wearing loose clothing, ties, jewellery and long hair that is not tied back

- the consumption of alcohol and non-prescription drugs and certain prescription drugs

- tampering with any guard or other safety device

- hurrying or cutting corners

- working with equipment unless already trained to do so.

2. A duty to:

- maintain a safe environment around a machine

- clean up spills and remove obstacles

- report defects or faults in equipment

- take simple precautions, such as not reaching into machines and following pre-start checks

- follow all safety instructions and procedures, including actions to be taken in the event of an unusual occurrence, such as a blockage in machinery.

Follow the manufacturer's instructions and recommendations

Information and training

People who operate work equipment and anyone else who may be affected must be made aware of the likely hazards involved – instructions, warnings and safety signs all play a part in this. Organisations must ensure that machine operators and people who clean, maintain or go near to machines are trained to use them safely and understand and carry out the appropriate safety precautions. Everyone must be made aware that it is not safe to operate or come into contact with a piece of machinery unless they have been trained and given permission to do so.

There must be careful supervision to ensure that the equipment is safe and that operators and others are following safe working procedures.

Key point

■ People operating machines must ensure that they:

- follow instructions and comply with safe working procedures

- do not wear loose clothing or jewellery

- tie up long hair and cover it

- report defects and faults immediately

- keep the working area clean and tidy

- switch off machines when not in use

- think about their safety and the safety of others and take care to prevent accidents

- do not use machines if they have been drinking alcohol or taking drugs

- do not tamper with guards or safety devices.

The use of personal protective equipment and clothing

Personal protective equipment and clothing (PPE/C) may need to be worn when using certain kinds of work equipment or when hazards cannot be controlled in other ways, such as when handling dangerous but essential chemicals. Organisations must select PPE/C carefully to ensure that it does not add to the risks – for example, by getting caught in machinery.

PPE/C should be used only as a last resort or as additional back up to other health and safety measures. As the hazard remains when PPE/C is in use, there could be severe consequences for health if the PPE/C does not function correctly, is put on incorrectly or is poorly maintained.

Risk assessments help employers and the self-employed to identify when they need to provide PPE/C and which PPE/C is the most appropriate for the task and environment.

Protective clothing

Special protective clothing can be used to protect the body from physical damage, chemicals, radiation and high and low temperatures. Examples are:

■ safety helmets for head protection

■ various types of clothing designed to protect against particular hazards, e.g. wet weather garments, high-visibility clothing, chemical-resistant garments, groin protectors and anti-static clothing

■ gloves to help to protect against cuts, hot and cold temperatures, chemicals, electricity and other hazards

■ footwear – possibly with special features such as anti-static materials or steel toe caps.

Respiratory protection

There are two main types of equipment for respiratory protection:

- masks and respirators – to filter contaminants, such as dust, from the air before they are inhaled

- breathing apparatus connected to a source of clean air – to supply air that is not contaminated by the immediate environment.

Eye protection

Eyes must be protected from dust, flying debris, chemicals and other hazards. Eye protection equipment includes safety glasses, goggles and face shields.

Safety helmets, and goggles can protect the head and eyes

The CE mark shows equipment complies with standards for design and manufacture

Hearing protection

Ear defenders or ear plugs may need to be worn in noisy areas or to reduce the likelihood of hearing damage or loss when noisy equipment is used (*see* Chapter 17).

Other protective equipment

Safety harnesses and other protective equipment may be necessary as a back up to other safety measures.

Selection and assessment

It is important to choose the correct type of PPE/C, so an assessment must be carried out to identify when it is needed and which type is most appropriate. Technical advice on suitability may be required. All protective equipment must:

- be suitable for the task and working environment

- give adequate personal protection

- fit properly and comfortably

- be compatible with other equipment used or worn

- have a CE mark to show that it complies with the necessary standards for design and manufacture.

Using PPE/C

All PPE/C must be properly used, maintained, cleaned and stored and it must be replaced when appropriate. If you need to use PPE/C, you must be provided with information, instruction, training and supervision to ensure that you understand the hazards and how to use, care for and store the equipment. To protect your own safety and that of others, you must follow instructions and report any defects or problems to your manager or supervisor.

Safety harnesses may be a necessary back up for other safety methods

Key points

■ PPE/C should be used only as a last resort when a hazard cannot be sufficiently controlled by other health and safety measures.

■ A range of PPE/C exists to protect various parts of the body, including eyes, ears, lungs, head, trunk, hands and feet.

■ The hazard remains when PPE/C is worn.

■ An assessment must be carried out to ensure that the correct PPE/C is provided.

■ Staff must be informed, instructed, trained and supervised to ensure that they understand the hazards, the need to wear their PPE/C and how to care for it.

Risk assessments

Before any equipment is installed or used, a risk assessment must be carried out. It should cover all the issues mentioned in this chapter and any others relevant to the work being carried out.

Maintenance, inspection and testing

Equipment, guards and safety devices must be checked regularly to ensure that they are in good working order. Only competent, qualified and, where necessary, named authorised persons must be permitted to inspect, test and maintain specific pieces of equipment. The recommendations of specialists about the safety of equipment must be followed.

Equipment must be checked regularly to ensure it is in good working order

Summary

1. The main dangers associated with machinery are entrapment, impact, contact, entanglement and ejection.

2. People operating machines must ensure that they:

- follow instructions and comply with safe working procedures
- do not wear loose clothing or jewellery
- tie up long hair and cover it
- report defects and faults immediately
- keep the working area clean and tidy
- switch off machines when not in use
- think about their safety and the safety of others and take care to prevent accidents
- do not use machines if they have been drinking alcohol or taking drugs
- do not tamper with guards or safety devices.

3. PPE/C should be used only as a last resort when a hazard cannot be sufficiently controlled by other health and safety measures.

4. A range of PPE/C exists to protect various parts of the body, including eyes, ears, lungs, head, trunk, hands and feet.

5. The hazard remains when PPE/C is worn.

6. An assessment must be carried out to ensure that the correct PPE/C is provided.

7. Staff must be informed, instructed, trained and supervised to ensure that they understand the hazards, the need to wear their PPE/C and how to care for it.

Chapter 12
Ergonomics and workstation design

Ergonomics is concerned with the interaction between people, equipment and their environment. Ergonomics should be considered when a new workplace is being designed, when new equipment is being selected and installed or when jobs and procedures are being considered. As employers become more aware of the human and financial costs associated with poorly designed workplaces and tasks, so the application of ergonomic principles increases.

Key words

Display screen equipment – equipment, such as a computer, with a visual display or monitor.

Ergonomics – the interaction between people, equipment and their environment.

Musculoskeletal disorders – conditions, often affecting the back, involving symptoms such as aches, pains, swelling and restricted movement.

Workstation – the arrangement of equipment, such as desks and production lines, at which people work.

WRULDs – work-related upper limb disorders affecting the neck, shoulders, arms and hands.

Design

It is a general principle of ergonomics that each workstation should be designed to suit the individual worker to improve his or her safety, comfort and productivity. However, as people range in height, shape and ability, it is normally uneconomic to design and create an individual workstation. Design must, therefore, reach a compromise and, wherever possible, should include adjustable features, such as seat height adjustment and adjustable platforms.

Musculoskeletal disorders

Poorly designed workstations and tasks may lead to musculoskeletal disorders causing aches, pain, swelling and poor performance. The back and arms are most commonly affected. Back problems may also be caused by lifting and carrying (*see* Chapter 13).

People may also be at risk from upper limb disorders – a variety of conditions affecting the arms, hands and upper body. Where problems are linked to tasks at work, they are called work-related upper limb disorders (WRULDs). People are more likely to have such problems if they:

- carry out a particular action repetitively
- use force
- maintain an awkward posture
- have inadequate rest periods.

People may be at risk in a variety of jobs – for example, repetitive factory, office or agricultural work. Where there are risks, employers should carry out a risk assessment of the tasks and seek expert advice if necessary. Where it is identified from risk assessment that there are safer or healthier ways of doing things, then employers will need to implement the recommendations from risk assessment. This needs to be undertaken through discussion and agreement with the people involved and some information and training will be needed.

Typical measures to help to prevent WRULDs include:

- re-designing workstations to reduce the risks caused by stooping, overreaching and similar actions
- reducing repetitive movements, such as by automation or job rotation
- reducing the force needed to carry out a task
- reducing stress levels, which may contribute to poor posture
- training staff in correct posture and safety precautions associated with the task
- making environmental improvements where possible, such as providing heating in cold areas.

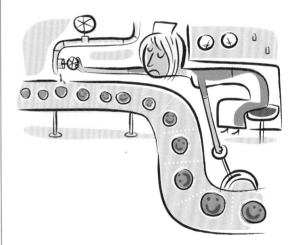

Key points

- Health problems may result from carrying out repetitive movements. These should be assessed and specific improvements made to prevent ill effects.

- Ergonomics can help to prevent a range of work-related complaints.

- Common techniques for preventing ill health involve reducing repetitive movements and the force required to do the task. Adequate breaks and rotation between jobs may also help.

Display screen equipment

Various ill effects, such as eyestrain, headaches and WRULDs, have been associated with jobs involving the use of display screens. Some of the methods that employers can take to prevent problems are:

- carrying out an assessment of the equipment and task and making any necessary improvements

- providing height-adjustable seats, with back rests and foot rests if needed

- allowing plenty of room for movement

- maintaining and selecting equipment, software and screen options to minimise flicker and reduce eye strain

- planning work to allow for breaks

- reducing stress levels

- reducing noise distractions

- providing appropriate training and information

- arranging for eye tests for certain staff.

Staff can also help to prevent health problems by, for example:

- sitting comfortably at the correct height with forearms parallel to the surface of the desktop and eyes level with the top of the screen

- maintaining a good posture

- avoiding repetitive and awkward movements by using a copy holder and keeping frequently used items within easy reach

- changing position regularly

- using a good keyboard and mouse technique with wrists straight and not using excessive force

- making sure there are no reflections or glare on screens by carefully positioning them in relation to sources of light

- adjusting the screen controls to prevent eye strain

- keeping the screen clean

- reporting to their manager any problems associated with use of the equipment.

Good posture and positioning can help to prevent health problems

Key points

- Everyone should be trained how to do their job. This should include information on how to reduce the risks, such as by improved workstation layout.

- Specific recommendations exist for those providing and using display screen equipment.

- Staff suffering from work-related aches and pains should report them to their employer for early attention.

Other uses for ergonomics

Ergonomics can assist with other issues, such as the layout of control panels on machines. Various aspects need to be considered; for example, the ability to reach emergency stop buttons and the clarity of controls and instructions.

The layout of control panels on machines can be ergonomically designed

Health problems – such as RSI – can result from repetitive movements

Summary

1. Health problems may result from carrying out repetitive movements. These should be assessed and specific improvements made to prevent ill effects.

2. Ergonomics can help to prevent a range of work-related complaints.

3. Common techniques for preventing ill health involve reducing repetitive movements and the force required to do the task. Adequate breaks and rotation between jobs may also help.

4. Everyone should be trained how to do their job. This should include information on how to reduce the risks, such as by improved workstation layout.

5. Specific recommendations exist for those providing and using display screen equipment.

6. Staff suffering from work-related aches and pains should report them to their employer for early attention.

Chapter 13
Manual handling

Almost one-third of reportable accidents results from handling, lifting and carrying activities. Virtually all workplaces have staff involved in some form of manual handling and the cost of injuries from poor or careless practice is extremely high.

Key words

Load – an object or person to be moved, held or positioned at work.

Manual handling – using the body to lift, carry, push or pull a load.

Reportable accident – one that must be reported to the appropriate enforcement authority.

Responsibilities of employers and employees

The Manual Handling Operations Regulations were introduced to try to reduce the number of employees being injured through lifting and moving loads at work. Under the Regulations, employers have to assess the risk of injury to employees from manual handling and – where practical – eliminate, automate or mechanise the movement of loads. Where this is not possible, employers have to consider the best way of moving loads with least risk to employees and ensure that employees are trained in manual handling and the methods devised.

Employees have to follow the training and methods devised by their employer and must not do anything that would put themselves or others at harm. Trying to do something that you know might injure or harm yourself, such as lifting something too heavy, is a legal offense under the Health and Safety at Work Act.

Mechanical aids can help to reduce the risk of manual handling injuries

Manual handling injuries

A variety of injuries may result from poor manual handling. These are most commonly to the back, but hands, arms and feet may also be damaged. Typical injuries include:

- ruptured discs
- sprained ligaments
- sprained and inflamed tendons
- muscular injuries
- trapped nerves
- hernias
- fractures
- cuts and crushing to parts of the body – for example, when a load is dropped onto fingers or feet.

Some injuries occur immediately, but many develop gradually. Most cause significant pain and result in absence from work.

Key points

- Typical manual handling injuries are back sprains and strains, cuts, bruises, crushing, fractures, hernias and trapped nerves.

- The effects of poor manual handling may not show immediately, so follow good procedures all the time to prevent a health problem developing.

Preventing injuries

As with other health and safety issues, the most effective method of prevention is to eliminate the hazard – in this case, to remove the need to carry out hazardous manual handling altogether. For example, it may be possible to re-design the workplace so that items do not need to be moved from one area to another. Alternatively, it may be possible to provide mechanical means, such as a conveyor belt, to move items. Any alternative means of moving objects must also be assessed and controlled to ensure that they do not cause injuries or other health problems.

Where manual handling tasks cannot be avoided, they must be assessed. This involves examining the tasks and deciding what the risks associated with them are and how these can be removed or reduced by adding control measures.

As part of a manual handling assessment, the following should be considered:

- the task to be carried out
- the load to be moved
- the environment in which handling takes place
- the capability of the individual involved in the manual handling.

A number of factors increase the risk of manual handling injuries, and these should be considered and controlled.

The task

To prevent injury:

1. Carry loads close to the body, because lifting and carrying with the load at arm's length increase the risk of injury.

2. Avoid awkward movements, such as stooping, reaching or twisting.

3. Ensure that the task is well designed and that procedures are followed.

4. Try to avoid lifting from the floor or to above shoulder height. Limit the distances for carrying. Mechanical aids may assist in reducing the force needed to move a load. These do not have to be complicated – a simple sack truck may help, but such aids must be used properly.

5. Minimise repetitive actions by re-designing and rotating tasks. Ensure that there are adequate rest periods and breaks between tasks.

6. Plan ahead – use teamwork where the load is too heavy for one person.

The load

To prevent injury:

1. Reduce the size and weight of loads to make handling easier. This could involve suppliers in packing items into smaller consignments before delivery.

2. Make loads easier to grasp and increase the stability of loads which may move suddenly and unpredictably.

3. Control harmful loads – for example, by covering sharp edges or by insulating hot containers.

4. Wear suitable PPE/C, such as non-slip gloves, safety footwear or overalls.

Reducing the weight of loads can make handling easier

Key point

■ Manual handling should be avoided wherever possible. Where it cannot be avoided, an assessment must be carried out and the handling task made safer by suitable control measures.

The environment

To prevent injury:

1. Ensure that the surroundings are safe – flooring should be even and not slippery, lighting should be adequate, and the temperature and humidity should be suitable.

2. Remove obstructions and ensure that the correct equipment is available.

The individual

To prevent injury:

1. Never attempt manual handling unless you have been trained and given permission to do so.

2. Ensure that you are capable of undertaking the task – people with health problems and pregnant women may be at particular at risk of injury.

Correct lifting procedure

As it is not possible to eliminate manual handling altogether, correct lifting procedures must be followed to minimise the risks of injury. The technique outlined below should be followed at home as well as at work.

Planning and preparation

1. Think about the task to be performed and plan the lift.

2. Consider what you will be lifting, where you will put it and how you are going to get there.

3. Assess the weight and centre of gravity of the load.

4. Assess the size of the load to make sure that you can grip it safely and see where you are going.

5. Assess whether you can lift the load safely without help. If not, get help. Bear in mind that it may be too dangerous to attempt to lift some loads, such as an office safe, even with a team.

6. If more than one person is involved, plan the lift first and agree who will lead and give instructions.

7. Plan your route and remove any obstructions. Check for any hazards, such as uneven flooring.

8. Avoid lifting unsafe loads, such as damaged glass or badly packed chemicals.

9. Check whether you need any PPE/C and obtain the necessary items, if appropriate. Check the equipment before use and check that it fits you.

10. Ensure that you will be able to maintain a firm grip.

11. Ensure that you are wearing the correct clothing, avoiding tight clothing and unsuitable footwear.

12. Remove any unnecessary packaging if this will make the task safer.

13. Consider a resting stage before moving a heavy load or carrying something any distance.

Position

1. Stand with your feet apart and your leading leg forward. Your weight should be even over both feet.

2. Position yourself (or turn the load around) so that the heaviest part is next to you. If the load is too far away, move toward it or bring it nearer before starting the lift.

Lift

Always lift using the correct posture:

1. Tuck the chin in on the way down.

2. Lean slightly forward if necessary and get a good grip.

3. Keep the shoulders level, without twisting or turning from the hips.

4. Try to grip with the hands around the base of the load.

5. Bring the load to waist height, keeping the lift as smooth as possible.

Move the load

1. Move the feet, keeping the load close to the body.

2. Proceed carefully, making sure that you can see where you are going.

Lower the load

1. Lower the load, reversing the procedure for lifting.

2. Avoid crushing fingers or toes as you put the load down.

3. Position and secure the load after putting it down.

Key point

- As it is not possible to eliminate manual handling, correct lifting procedures must be followed to minimise the risk of injury.

 Stand with your feet apart and weight distributed evenly. Keep shoulders level and grip the base of the load

 Bring the load up to waist height, keep the load close to your body

 When lowering the load, reverse the procedure for lifting and avoid crushing fingers when you put the load down

Dealing with problems

Report any problems, such as strains and sprains, immediately. Where there are changes – for example, to the activity or the load – the task must be reassessed.

Summary

1. Typical manual handling injuries are back sprains and strains, cuts, bruises, crushing, fractures, hernias and trapped nerves.

2. The effects of poor manual handling may not show immediately, so follow good procedures all the time to prevent a health problem developing.

3. Manual handling should be avoided wherever possible. Where it cannot be avoided, an assessment must be carried out and the handling task made safer by suitable control measures.

4. As it is not possible to eliminate manual handling, correct lifting procedures must be followed to minimise the risk of injury.

Chapter 14
Hazardous substances

Hazardous substances are used in many workplaces and may lead to a range of conditions, including dermatitis, asthma and infectious diseases. Visitors and the general public may be at risk from hazardous substances, as well as the person using them.

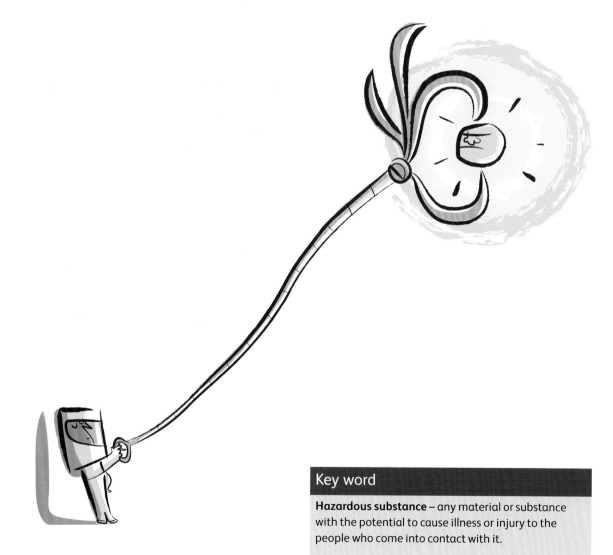

Key word

Hazardous substance – any material or substance with the potential to cause illness or injury to the people who come into contact with it.

Types of hazardous substance

Hazardous substances include anything that could cause ill health to people who come into contact with them. There are many reasons why a substance may be hazardous – for example, it may be:

- explosive or inflammable
- associated with a dangerous chemical reaction
- toxic, corrosive, harmful or irritating to parts of the human body
- the cause of diseases or allergies.

Hazardous substances come in many forms, including:

- **liquid** – for example, cleaning chemicals
- **dust** – for example, lead and asbestos
- **fumes** – for example, from industrial chemicals
- **gases** – for example, carbon monoxide
- **living organisms** – for example, fungal spores.

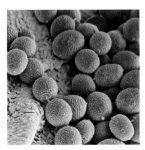

A substance may be hazardous for a number of reasons – it may be explosive

Hazardous substances include living organisms, such as fungal spores

Routes of entry

There are a number of ways in which hazardous substances can enter the body:

- **absorption** – where a hazardous substance gets onto the skin and is absorbed through it into the body and bloodstream
- **ingestion** – through swallowing a hazardous substance or where one might be splashed into the mouth
- **inhalation** – through breathing in a hazardous substance, such as toxic fumes
- **injection** – where a sharp object, such as a needle, has a hazardous substance on it and cuts or punctures the skin.

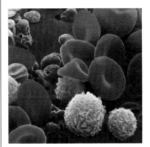

Hazardous substances can enter the body by a number of routes including absorption from the skin into the bloodstream

Key point

- Hazardous substances can cause a wide range of health problems, such as dermatitis and asthma. They may also cause other problems, such as explosions or fires.

Prevention of accidents and ill health

The best method of preventing accidents and ill health from hazardous substances is to avoid using or storing them altogether. Where this is not possible, an assessment must be carried out and appropriate control measures put in place to reduce the risks to an acceptable level.

Identifying hazardous substances

It is important to identify substances that could cause harm. Purchased substances must be in their original containers and have safety labels and safety information. If dangerous chemicals have to be decanted before use, they should be poured into containers approved by the manufacturer and labelled appropriately.

Other sources of information, such as government literature, may also need to be consulted.

Assessing the risks

Companies must assess the risks from all hazardous substances used or created. The person carrying out the assessment must have the necessary legal and technical knowledge as well as access to the correct information. In some cases, this may mean obtaining specialist expertise.

The assessor should read the suppliers' safety data sheets and consider various issues, such as:

■ how hazardous the substance is

■ how much is used

■ how often it is used

■ whether levels exceed government limits.

When an assessment is thorough, a range of details is considered, covering all eventualities. Assessments should be reviewed at regular intervals or when updating is needed – for example, when changes are made to processes or materials used.

Preventing exposure

Exposure should be prevented whenever possible by avoiding the need for, or production of, hazardous substances. Safer substances should be substituted.

Controlling exposure

Various techniques can be used to reduce risks even where hazardous substances are used; for example by:

■ enclosing a process

■ using local and general ventilation

■ using safe systems of work and good housekeeping to minimise spills and leaks

■ reducing the number of people and time for which people are exposed

■ using suitable PPE/C.

The controls chosen must be checked on a regular basis to make sure that they are performing efficiently. In some cases, the levels of hazardous substances in the air must be monitored. Staff must report any defects in control measures to managers immediately.

When hazardous substances are used, exposure must be controlled

Key points

■ The best method of preventing accidents and ill health is to avoid using, storing and creating hazardous substances altogether.

■ Where hazardous substances have to be used, a full assessment must be carried out.

■ Prevention or control measures must be used to minimise the risks of injury or ill health.

ACME
SUCK-O-MAT

Health surveillance

Staff working with some hazardous substances need regular health checks – for example, to check the skin for dermatitis or the functioning of the lungs.

Information and training procedures

All employees should be given information, instruction and training to ensure that they are aware of hazards and the risks and know which precautions to take. In particular, staff must know how to operate the control measures, use PPE/C and take appropriate action in an emergency.

It is important for safe working procedures to be established and followed carefully. Quite often, simple procedures can prevent injury and illness:

Never

- mix different chemicals together

- decant chemicals to unlabelled or incorrectly-labelled containers

- never use chemicals you are not trained and authorised to use.

Always

- use the correct PPE/C

- report any defects or operational problems, such as poor ventilation

- keep your workplace clean and tidy

- avoid blocking walkways, to prevent tripping while handling chemicals

- store chemicals in a secure area

- report any symptoms of ill health immediately.

Key points

- People working with hazardous substances must be properly informed and trained in how to use substances safely.

- Staff should report any health problems or defects to control measures or personal PPE/C immediately.

- Always follow the safety rules of your workplace.

Supply, transport and large-scale storage

Additional stringent safety measures are necessary in these cases to ensure the health and safety of users and the general public. For example, suppliers must label goods and provide appropriate information, while haulage companies must consider the additional risks posed by the movement of dangerous substances.

Safety signs should be used to indicate dangerous substances

Summary

1. Hazardous substances can cause a wide range of health problems, such as dermatitis and asthma. They may also cause other problems, such as explosions or fires.

2. The best method of preventing accidents and ill health is to avoid using, storing and creating hazardous substances altogether.

3. Where hazardous substances have to be used, a full assessment must be carried out.

4. Prevention or control measures must be used to minimise the risks of injury or ill health.

5. People working with hazardous substances must be properly informed and trained in how to use substances safely.

6. Staff should report any health problems or defects to control measures or PPE/C immediately.

7. Always follow the safety rules of your workplace.

Chapter 15
Working at height

Working at height can be dangerous and is the biggest cause of fatal accidents at work to employees and the self-employed. Most people work at height from time to time even if the height is not very high. Specific regulations apply to working at height and there are a number of precautions employers and employees need to take.

Working at height accidents

A variety of situations can result in falls from height. The most common ones are:

- using ladders – this might be for a simple job, such as cleaning windows or cleaning out gutters

- working on scaffolding and other access equipment – used extensively in the construction industry and for building repair work

- going onto roofs or into roof spaces to clean or carry out maintenance work

- using chairs or other unsuitable means of gaining access to places that are not very high but cannot be reached from the ground

- falling through ceilings and fragile roofs

- materials and objects falling from where people are working at height and striking persons below.

Using ladders, working on scaffolding or on roofs or in roof spaces can be dangerous

Key point

- The main risk of working at height is falling.

The main reasons for falling from height accidents

As with most accidents, there are a number of common reasons and factors that contribute to working at height accidents. Some common ones include:

- not having a safe system of work in place
- not following a safe system of work
- not recognising the risk of working at height
- not providing proper information, instruction and training
- not providing the proper equipment for the job.

Accidents can often be caused by the simplest things. In the case of ladders, this includes over stretching, placing the ladder incorrectly and not securing it properly. Other accidents involve carrying loads and slipping off ladders due to unsuitable footwear being worn.

General precautions

All instances of working at height require some thought as to how it should be carried out safely. Some general principles apply:

1. Assess the risk of working at height.

2. Plan the job – decide on the safest way to do it after considering all the circumstances, including the environment, height, duration, tasks and means of escape in an emergency.

3. Select the right equipment for the job.

4. Select the right people for the job – those that are competent, have experience and have been trained.

5. Supervise the job to ensure that it is done as planned.

6. Consider using fall arrest equipment, such as harnesses.

7. Frequently check the equipment to ensure that it is working properly and is safe.

Key points

- All jobs – where there is a risk of injury from falling – must be risk assessed and planned in order to reduce the risk.
- All equipment involved in working at height must be:
  - appropriate for the job
  - in good working order, with no damage or defects
  - on a sound, level surface
  - used by competent people.
- People must be trained, know what they are doing and know the correct procedure to follow when working at height.

Equipment for working at height

A variety of access equipment is available for working at height. The most common ones are:

- ladders and stepladders
- scaffolds
- mobile towers
- elevating work platforms.

Ladders and stepladders

Although very useful and often essential, ladders and stepladders are often used incorrectly. Ladders should be provided to gain *access* to workplaces and should not normally be used as the workplace. Ladders and stepladders should only be used for short and simple tasks. Consideration should first be given to the use of an alternative to ladders, such as a mobile towers, elevating work platforms or scaffold. If, however, ladders have to be used, then the following rules should be followed:

1. Only use ladders that are sound, with no damage or defects. Anyone using a ladder needs to check for damage or defects.

2. Ladders need to be set at the correct angle of 75 degrees (4 up for every 1 out) to prevent the risk of slippage or falling.

3. Ladders need to be secured or tied at the top end and secured or 'footed' at the bottom by someone holding the ladder.

4. Ladders must only be placed on sound, level surfaces.

Ladders should only be used to complete short, simple tasks

Position the ladder correctly – do not overstretch

Scaffolds

Scaffolds are designed for people to work safely at height. However, there are many accidents that involve such scaffolding and these accidents sometimes involve the people who erect and dismantle it. All working platforms need to be:

- stable and on firm footings
- of sufficient strength for the job and loads to be placed on them
- erected by competent persons and inspected frequently by a competent person
- provided with barriers/handrails at the working level to prevent persons falling
- provided with edge protection or toe boards to prevent objects falling from the working platform
- provided with safe means of access
- provide for materials to be safely stacked
- fully boarded out to provide a safe platform.

Scaffolding should be fully boarded to provide a safe platform

Mobile towers

Mobile towers can be quickly erected and moved from place to place. Mobile towers should often be used in place of ladders as they provide a much more stable and secure place to work. The following rules apply when using mobile towers:

1. Follow the manufacturers' instructions for erection and dismantling.

2. Make sure that the tower is on a level and firm surface (the tower is vertical) and that the wheels are locked.

3. Provide a safe means of access and egress – normally via an internal ladder.

4. Provide toe boards and guard rails.

5. Ensure that the maximum load is not exceeded.

6. Ensure that only trained persons use the platform and supervise them.

7. Only move the tower when no-one is on it and loads have been removed.

8. When moving the tower, check the ground and watch for anything overhead – for example, power lines.

9. Never climb up the outside of a tower as it might tip over.

Mobile towers can provide a stable and secure place to work

Elevating work platforms

Elevating work platforms can provide very good and safe access to working at height, but like all other pieces of equipment, there are some key safety features that need to be in place:

1. Only trained and competent staff must operate the equipment.

2. The working platform (like a low-level cage) should be provided with toe boards and a barrier to prevent a person from falling.

3. The equipment should be used only on a level and firm surface.

4. Emergency procedures must be in place.

5. Tyres should be properly inflated.

6. Dangerous parts should be properly guarded.

7. Warning signs and notices must be displayed to warn others that people are working overhead/ at height.

Warning signs and notices must be displayed when working at height

Key points

■ A variety of access equipment is available for working at height – ladders, scaffolding, mobile towers and elevating work platforms. It is important that the right access equipment is chosen for the job.

■ People must be trained, know what they are doing and the correct procedure to follow when working at height.

Summary

1. The main risk of working at height is falling.

2. All jobs – where there is a risk of injury from falling must be risk assessed and planned in order to reduce the risk.

3. All equipment involved in working at height must be:

- appropriate for the job

- in good working order, with no damage or defects

- on a sound, level surface

- used by competent people.

4. A variety of access equipment is available for working at height – ladders, scaffolding, mobile towers and elevating work platforms. It is important that the right access equipment is chosen for the job.

5. People must be trained, know what they are doing and the correct procedure to follow when working at height.

Chapter 16
Transport and vehicles

The movement of goods and people at work in transport and vehicles is the second greatest cause of fatal accidents at work. It also accounts for over 1,000 serious injuries each year. The causes of accidents and injury to drivers and passengers are normally from collisions, overturning or impact. Pedestrians are injured most often by being struck or knocked over by vehicles or being struck by loads falling from vehicles. Reversing vehicles can be a particular hazard.

Key words

Pedestrians – anyone on foot, including employees, contractors, visitors and the public.

Traffic routes – the specific marked areas to be used for workplace vehicles.

Workplace transport – includes vehicles used in or around workplaces, such as fork-lift trucks, delivery vans, dumper trucks.

Causes of work transport and vehicle accidents

There are a number of common reasons and factors associated with work transport and vehicle accidents, which include:

- using the wrong vehicle or an unsuitable vehicle for the job

- driver error, sometimes due to poor training and lack of competence

- driver error due to tiredness resulting from working long hours

- driving too fast

- using the vehicle in the wrong area, such as on slopes leading to overturning (often associated with driving too fast)

- poorly maintained or defective vehicles – for example, brakes or warning hazards not working properly

- misuse of vehicles and horseplay.

As with other areas of health and safety, most transport and vehicle accidents are preventable. There are three main areas to consider:

- the workplace

- drivers

- the vehicle.

Key point

- Workplace transport and vehicles can cause fatal and serious accidents.

The workplace

The workplace can be designed and maintained so as to minimise the risk of accidents and injury due to transport activities and vehicles. Some of the main ways to reduce the risk include:

- planning traffic routes and providing a one-way system if possible

- providing marked parking areas or bays for vehicles

- trying to avoid blind or sharp bends on traffic routes

- ensuring that traffic routes are wide enough for vehicles and for turning where needed

- ensuring that surfaces are level and well maintained

- providing safe areas for loading and unloading

- ensuring that traffic routes are well marked and signed

- providing adequate lighting for all traffic routes, which includes lighting for night and evening working or in areas where there is poor natural light

- gritting roads and traffic routes in icy conditions to try to reduce the risk of skidding and sliding

- ensuring that traffic routes are free from obstructions and other hazards and away from such things as chemical or gas tanks.

Key point

- Traffic routes and movements need to be planned following an assessment of the risks.

Drivers

Whatever is being driven, anyone using vehicles needs to be trained and competent to use them. For some types of vehicles, such as fork-lift trucks, this means passing a test of competence to demonstrate being able to drive safely before being allowed to use the vehicle. Some of the basic rules include:

1. Testing drivers' competence or ensuring that they have the right experience, qualifications or a certificate – instruction and training will nearly always be required.

2. Selecting and authorising named drivers only.

3. Checking that drivers follow the rules, use the correct routes and keep to speed limits. Like other areas of health and safety, drivers need to be supervised and managed properly.

4. Ensuring that drivers have sufficient time to do any job safely (to avoid them rushing).

5. Ensuring that drivers take breaks and that work patterns are such that they do not become overtired and increase the risk of making mistakes.

In addition to employees, it is often visitors or other company drivers who may be making a delivery that cause the greatest risk. Employers need to ensure that those drivers also follow the rules and routes and drive safely. This may mean providing them with the rules and information on how to move around safely, speed limits and where to report and park. Keys should not be left in parked vehicles so as to prevent the risk of unauthorised use.

Drivers must take breaks

The vehicle

Appropriate vehicles need to be provided that are suitable for the job to be done. Once in use, they need to be maintained in good working order and be checked regularly for faults and defects. The main points about vehicles and their safety include:

- suitability for the work and the environment
- safe means for the driver to get in and out of the vehicle
- good visibility (all round if possible)
- horn, vehicles lights and other warning devices, such as a reversing alarm, being present and working
- guarding of dangerous moving parts
- protecting the driver from adverse weather conditions or from other environmental factors, such as rain, wind and dust
- seat belts or other form of securing the driver safely in the case of an accident or sudden stop
- driver protection from overturning.

Before vehicles are put into service, they need to be checked. A number of checks should also be made before a driver uses a vehicle, such as:

- brakes
- steering
- tyres
- alarms and warning devices
- mirrors and windscreen wipers
- instruments
- any damage to the vehicle.

Key point

- Vehicles need to be properly selected, maintained and used following safe procedures.

Preventing pedestrian accidents

Being hit by a moving vehicle is very serious, causing either death or serious injury to a pedestrian. There are a number of ways to protect persons from injury from moving vehicles:

1. Keep vehicles and pedestrians separated as much and as far apart as possible and provide each with safe routes and safe access.

2. Provide physical barriers so that it is difficult for vehicles to stray into pedestrian areas.

3. Mark routes so that it is clear where vehicles and pedestrians are allowed to go.

4. Display signs and warning notices to remind people of the rules.

5. Provide safe marked places for pedestrians to cross over traffic routes.

6. Ensure that there is a safe speed limit set for workplaces and enforce the limit.

7. Ensure that vehicles are maintained and that everything is working properly.

Keep vehicles and pedestrians separated to prevent accidents

Key point

■ Pedestrians and vehicles need to be kept apart/separated as much as possible.

Reversing vehicles

Reversing a vehicle carries a specific risk that must be controlled to ensure that pedestrians are not run over. Reversing needs to be kept to a minimum, but where there is the need for reversing, such as in delivery areas or bays, the following should apply:

■ mark reversing areas

■ ensure that vehicles have audible and visual warning, where possible, to alert people to the reversing vehicle

■ limit or restrict the people that are allowed in reversing areas

■ have someone responsible on the ground to assist the vehicle driver in reversing

■ ensure that the vehicle is fitted with side-mounted and rear-view mirrors to assist the driver to see properly

■ ensure that reversing speed limits are very low

■ put up visible warning notices

■ ensure that there is sufficient space for safe reversing

Legal requirements

Workplace transport and vehicles can be subject to a number of general legal requirements and some more specific ones. However, risk assessments need to include transport and vehicle safety, which is also covered by the Provision and Use of Work Equipment Regulations 1998.

Summary

1. Workplace transport and vehicles can cause many serious and fatal accidents.

2. Traffic routes and movements need to be planned following an assessment of the risks.

3. Only competent persons should drive workplace vehicles, which often means providing training and instruction.

4. Vehicles need to be properly selected, maintained and used following safe procedures.

5. Pedestrians and vehicles need to be kept apart/separated as much as possible.

Chapter 17
Noise and vibration

Exposure to excessive noise can cause hearing damage and even loss, the effects from which may be cumulative and irreversible. Noise also interferes with communication, can cause distraction and may, therefore, compromise safety. Designers, importers, suppliers, manufacturers, employers, employees and the self-employed all have obligations towards noise control and the protection of hearing.

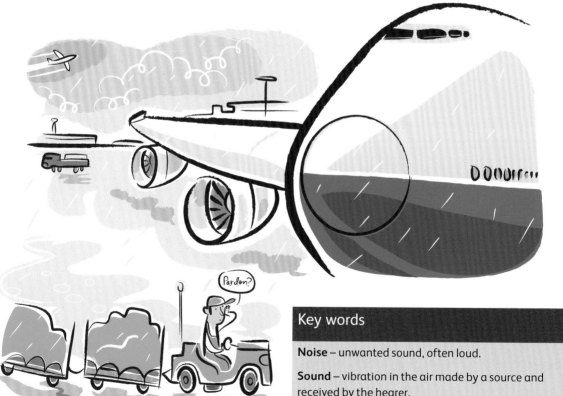

Key words

Noise – unwanted sound, often loud.

Sound – vibration in the air made by a source and received by the hearer.

Tinnitus – a medical condition involving ringing in the ears.

Vibration – the small but rapid and repetitive movement of, for example, a piece of work equipment.

Sources of noise

Noise is produced by people and many types of equipment, including printers, vehicles, radios and motors. It can cause a nuisance or stress. Where noise is very loud, it may cause hearing damage or loss of hearing. The level of risk is linked to the amount of sound energy to which the ear is exposed.

Noise is controlled by legislation that requires employers to protect the hearing of people affected by the noise from work. At a certain level, where hearing damage will occur if exposed for a sustained period, employers have to ensure that all persons in that area wear ear defenders.

Excessive noise over a period of time can cause tinnitus, which is a ringing in the ears. This can sometimes be felt temporarily when exposed to hours of noise, such as when at a pop concert. The ringing in the ears eventually subsides after a few hours and is known as temporary threshold shift. If exposure continues for a long time, permanent damage is done to the hearing hair cells, which can cause continued tinnitus and loss of hearing at certain frequencies.

Risk assessment

To determine whether noise in an area is likely to cause damage to hearing, noise readings need to be taken. These noise surveys must be carried out by suitably qualified and experienced personnel using specialist equipment. Noise is measured in decibels (dB) and readings are taken throughout the day/week to determine the average level of noise and to identify which periods are particularly loud. There are levels of noise exposure that must not be exceeded (a daily or weekly exposure of 87dB).

Some levels of noise (currently between 80 – 85dB) may cause damage to the ear and employers have to provide hearing protection. It is the responsibility of the employee to decide whether to use hearing protection or not – unless the employer decides that it is necessary at that level.

If daily or weekly noise exposure exceeds 85dB, hearing protection is mandatory.

In addition to average noise, where there is sudden impact noise over a certain level or short bursts of loud noise over a period, it may again be necessary for persons in the area to use hearing protection.

Noise is measured in decibels (dB) – the daily exposure limit is 87dB

Controls

The risks from exposure to noise must be reduced as far as is reasonably practicable and a number of control measures can be considered.

Everyone has responsibilities for noise, although the individual responsible for each control varies. The controls include:

- design and layout that takes into account the source of noise and the relative position of people

- purchasing quieter equipment or using quieter processes or silencers

- enclosing the source of the noise with sound-absorbing materials

- screening noisy processes

- lagging noisy pipework

- providing acoustic wall or ceiling panels

- isolating staff in noise-protected areas

- controlling the time that individuals are exposed to noise

- maintaining equipment and machinery, including lubrication

- providing hearing protection (ear defenders or plugs).

The best controls are those that reduce the amount of noise being produced, followed by enclosure and noise proofing. As a last resort, hearing protection may need to be worn.

Hearing protection should be used as a last resort

Personal protective equipment

Hearing protection prevents some of the sound energy reaching the ear and should be used when noise cannot be reduced by other measures. Ear defenders and plugs must be:

- selected carefully – expert advice may be required

- fitted correctly

- compatible with other forms of PPE/C, such as bump hats and goggles

- properly looked after

- worn whenever it is appropriate.

There should be signs to indicate areas where hearing protection is needed. Staff who are affected must be appropriately informed, instructed, trained and supervised.

Signs should be used to indicate where hearing protection is needed

Key points

- In noisy environments, assessments need to be carried out by suitably qualified personnel and the noise controlled to reduce risks.

- Training and supervision must be provided for staff working in noisy areas or carrying out noisy activities.

- Personal protective equipment designed to protect hearing must be selected carefully and looked after with care.

- Ear defenders or plugs must always be worn in designated noisy areas.

Vibration

The body can be harmed through excess exposure to vibration. Most commonly this is by using hand-held vibrating power tools, such as drills and grinders. If used for too long over a period of time, it can cause pain in the muscles, nerves and bones of the arms and hands. It is often referred to as vibration white finger (VWF). Such conditions needs to be reported immediately.

To prevent harm from vibration, it is best to avoid using vibrating tools and find another way to do the job. However, if vibrating tools are needed, then their use should be kept to a minimum. Good maintenance of equipment helps to reduce the amount of vibration.

Vibrating equipment and tools are often a source of noise, which can be a problem to the user in addition to the vibration itself. Because of the closeness of the equipment to the operator, one of the few controls is the use of ear defenders.

Key point

■ Vibration can cause harm through continued exposure and needs to be controlled as with any risk.

Summary

1. Excessive noise can cause hearing loss and damage and can impair general communication.

2. In noisy environments, assessments need to be carried out by suitably qualified personnel and the noise controlled to reduce risks.

3. Training and supervision must be provided for staff working in noisy areas or carrying out noisy activities.

4. Personal protective equipment designed to protect hearing must be selected carefully and looked after with care.

5. Ear defenders or plugs must always be worn in designated noisy areas.

6. Vibration can cause harm through continued exposure and needs to be controlled as with any risk.

Index

Design: www.red-stone.com
Illustration: Ned Jolliffe
Photography: Andrew Olney

Except pages 13T (Shout/Alamy), 13B (Shout/Alamy), 15T (CNRI/Science Photo
Library, 15B (SuperStock/Alamy), 18B (Bernd Auers/Photonica/Getty Images),
21 (Steve Cole/Photodisc Red/Getty Images), 27T (Image Source/Punchstock),
27B (Stockbyte Platinum/Alamy), 28T (Image100/Getty Images), 28B (Image Farm
Inc./Alamy), 31L (Pixoi Ltd/Alamy), 34 (Stockbyte/Stockbyte Gold/Getty Images),
37 (Tim Hall/Photodisc Red/Getty Images), 39B (Michael Donne/ Science Photo
Library), 40L (SuperStock/Alamy), 40RT (Shout/Alamy), 40RB (Cordelia Molloy/Science
Photo Library), 43B (Bluestone/Science Photo Library), 47 (Dorling Kindersley/Getty
Images), 48 (Stockbyte Platinum/Alamy), 52R (Paul Whitehill/Science Photo Library),
56 (Rob Casey/Alamy), 59T (Stockdisc/Punchstock), 59MT (D Falconer/PhotoLink/
Photodisc Green/Getty Images), 59MB (Powered by Light/Alan Spencer/Alamy),
59B (Stockbyte Platinum/Alamy), 61T (Thomas Tolstrup/Nordic Photos/Getty Images),
61B (Alan Thornton/The Image Bank/Getty Images), 65T (David Potter/ Construction
Photography), 66L (Frances M. Roberts/Alamy), 70 (Computing Plus, Oxford, UK),
71T (John Coletti/Photodisc Green/Getty Images), 71B (Jacky Chapman/Alamy),
79LT (Don Smetzer/Stone/Getty Images), 79LB (Steve Gschmeissner/Science Photo
Library), 79R (National Cancer Institute/Science Photo Library), 81 (Steve Taylor/
Digital Vision/Getty Images), 85T (Manor Photography/Alamy), 85B (Nick Dolding/
Taxi/Getty Images), 87R (David De Lossy/Photodisc Green/Getty Images),
88 (L–R) (David Potter/ Construction Photography), 92 (Eye Candy Images/Alamy),
94 (Shout/Alamy), 97 Kampfner Photography/Alamy), 98L (Ashley Cooper/Alamy),
98R (Robert Brook/Science Photo Library).

Shoot location: Beacon Press, Uckfield, Sussex

Print: RR Donnelley